BOOKS IN THE SPECIAL EDUCATION SERIES

Donald H. Painting, Ph.D., completed his undergraduate studies at the University of Rochester and his graduate work in clinical psychology at the University of Kentucky. He is clinical director of the Pathway School in Audubon, Pennsylvania, an adjunct faculty member of Eastern College in St. Davids, Pennsylvania, an editorial advisor of Perceptions, Inc., and he is in part-time private practice.

Prentice-Hall International, Inc., *London*
Prentice-Hall of Australia Pty. Limited, *Sydney*
Prentice-Hall Canada Inc., *Toronto*
Prentice-Hall of India Private Limited, *New Delhi*
Prentice-Hall of Japan, Inc., *Tokyo*
Prentice-Hall of Southeast Asia Pte. Ltd., *Singapore*
Whitehall Books Limited, *Wellington, New Zealand*
Editora Prentice-Hall do Brasil Ltda., *Rio de Janeiro*

Donald H. Painting

Helping Children with Specific Learning Disabilities
A PRACTICAL GUIDE FOR PARENTS AND TEACHERS

A SPECTRUM BOOK

Prentice-Hall, Inc., Englewood Cliffs, New Jersey 07632

Library of Congress Cataloging in Publication Data

Painting, Donald H.
    Helping children with specific learning
disabilities.

    (Special education series)
    "A Spectrum Book."
    Bibliography: p.
    Includes index.
    1. Learning disabilities.   I. Title.
II. Series.
LC4704.P34 1983   371.91'4   82-13258
ISBN 0-13-387258-0
ISBN 0-13-387241-6 (pbk.)

To the
Association for Children with Learning Disabilities,
*which provides an invaluable service
for learning disabled children and their parents.*

This book is available at a special discount when ordered in
bulk quantities. Contact Prentice-Hall, Inc., General Publishing Division,
Special Sales, Englewood Cliffs, New Jersey 07632.

1 2 3 4 5 6 7 8 9 10

ISBN 0-13-387258-0

ISBN 0-13-387241-6 {PBK.}

Editorial/production supervision by Chris McMorrow
Cover design © 1983 by Jeannette Jacobs
Manufacturing buyer: Cathie Lenard

Contents

PRINCIPLES OF BEHAVIOR MANAGEMENT

REKINDLE THE FLAME

Preface

Many labels and definitions are used to describe the symptoms and nature of a specific learning disability (SLD). These terms can be vague, specific, or partially overlapping. This lack of uniform terminology in the literature is confusing when trying to understand what may be wrong with a child, what causes the symptoms, and what can be done about them. Regardless of the terminology, parents and teachers of an SLD child recognize very quickly the drain on their resources to cope with that child. This perpetual drain on parents and teachers can eventually make them feel completely depleted of patience, energy, hope, and motivation to keep trying.

This book provides parents, teachers, and other professionals with a basis for recognizing and understanding the symptoms of specific learning disabilities, as well as developing effective behavior management techniques. Behavioral deviations are discussed from a developmental viewpoint. Descriptive vignettes illustrate typical behavior patterns of SLD children, and problem behaviors are explained in terms of underlying skill weaknesses. Basic principles of behavior management are presented along with practical recommendations, community resources, annotated bibli-ography, and glossary. Boldface words in the text are defined in the glossary. Although a sexist approach is certainly not intended, the pro-nouns "his" or "her" will be used throughout the text to prevent the excessive verbiage of saying "his/her" every time a pronoun is used.

Deep appreciation is extended to the many students who have attended the Pathway School in Audubon, Pennsylvania, along with their families and Pathway's professional staff. Years of clinical experience with these individuals provided the inspiration, insights, and determination to write this book.

Introduction
Both Sides
of the Story

chapter one

Children with **specific learning disabilities** display a variety of symptoms. Some experience problems primarily with academic subjects and are unable to read, spell, or handle mathematics at the expected level for their mental ability and chronological age. Other children experience problems primarily in the development of speech and language skills. They mispronounce words, have difficulty understanding the meaning of what they hear, or are unable to communicate their thoughts in spoken language in age-appropriate ways. Still other children experience problems with coordination and are awkward and clumsy when eating, running, catching a ball, or performing other similar activities. Others have problems with attention and concentration, memory, or reasoning abilities.

Generally speaking, each child with a specific learning disability experiences problems in more than one area. No one child necessarily has all the characteristics of a specific learning disability, nor is there a particular pattern of characteristics that is similar for most of these children. A significant percentage of these children do experience problems with self-confidence and self-control, however, which is the focus of this book. For information and guidance concerning academic, speech and language, or coordination problems, refer to the books listed in the Bibliography by

Adamson and Adamson, Battin, Consilia, Cruickshank, Hammill and Bartel, Haring and Bateman, Rosner, Valett, and Weiss and Lillywhite.

In conjunction with Public Law 94-142, The Education for All Handicapped Children Act of 1975, the federal government established definitions for the various types of conditions which produce a handicap for which special education techniques are needed. A specific learning disability (SLD) is defined as

> . . . a disorder in one or more of the basic psychological processes involved in understanding or in using language, spoken or written, which may manifest itself in an imperfect ability to listen, think, speak, read, write, spell, or to do mathematical calculations. The term includes such conditions as **perceptual handicaps, brain injury, minimal brain dysfunction, dyslexia,** and **developmental aphasia.** The term does not include children who have learning problems which are primarily the result of visual, hearing, or **motor handicaps,** of **mental retardation,** or of environmental, cultural, or economic disadvantage.*

Unfortunately, this definition makes no mention of the social and emotional adjustment problems that almost inevitably accompany a specific learning disability. While children might develop similar symptoms of social and emotional problems for different reasons, the existence of a specific learning disability is certainly one of them. These adjustment problems vary from disruptive, aggressive, and destructive behaviors to avoidance of tasks, a subtle lack of cooperation, and shyness. Usually these adjustment problems are inseparable from the learning problems and even further impair each SLD child's ability to handle daily experiences successfully.

It is also unfortunate that many public school systems have decided to restrict the classification of specific learning disabilities to include learning disabled children who demonstrate at least average intelligence. The symptoms of a specific learning disability generally impairs the effectiveness of a child's intellectual functioning. In spite of average or higher intellectual potential, a child with a specific learning disability might perform at various levels below average, depending upon the severity of the symptoms. Such a child may even be functioning at the mentally deficient level, but his erratic or uneven skill levels will frequently reflect higher potential ability.

*Public Law 94-142: "Education of Handicapped Children," *Federal Register* 42, no. 163, Tuesday, August 23, 1977, 42478.

The child with a specific learning disability typically presents a complex, confusing, and perplexing puzzle. Not the kind that can be solved in one evening, but the kind that requires years of effort. After working with the puzzle day after day, month after month, and year after year, parents and teachers experience a spectrum of reactions. They have decreasing amounts of optimism, patience, energy, and enthusiasm, and increasing amounts of anger, resentment, hurt, guilt, and frustration. Although parents and teachers may try hard to control these negative reactions, their controls do not always work, which only increases the complexity of the puzzle.

On the other hand, the SLD child experiences his own set of unpleasant feelings, many of which are very similar to those experienced by parents and teachers. After all, it is the child's life that is most directly involved. The child has to live with his problems and feelings twenty-four hours a day.

Each day can become a dreaded experience. Teachers look forward to the end of each school day; parents look forward to evening when their child is asleep; the SLD child takes solace in the daily activities that are least demanding and frustrating.

UNDERSTANDING "WHY" SOMETIMES HELPS

When parents and teachers of an SLD child have to deal with the child's maladaptive, disruptive, perhaps even "strange" behavior each day, they may very quickly show signs of wear. The atmosphere becomes oppressive and tense: tempers are short, moods are irritable, and beneath all this the adults are often anxious and confused. It is normal to fear the unknown or feel apprehensive about the unexplained. An unpleasant situation becomes more tolerable, however, if we at least have some understanding of why it exists, even if the situation does not improve significantly.

Variations of Normal Child Development

Probably most if not all the behaviors displayed by the SLD child have been displayed at one time or another by every normal child in the course of growing up. In that sense, the SLD child's behavior is really not "strange," unique, or particularly abnormal. For example, it is not unusual for most children at one time or another to have a temper tantrum, to daydream, or to be stubborn, provocative, or forgetful. Parents of normal children have their moments of concern and irritation, of course, but qualitatively it is not the same as when these same kinds of behavior occur with an SLD child. There are at least three reasons why the SLD child's behavior is so much more upsetting for parents and teachers, is more difficult to manage, is often considered to be unusual or "strange."

First, the SLD child displays problem behavior more frequently than a "normal" child. A normal child may have a temper tantrum once a week or less, whereas an SLD child may have a temper tantrum once a day or more. The increased frequency of problem behavior makes it almost intolerable for the adult to cope with after a while. The adult's energy is depleted faster than it can be replenished.

Second, the SLD child typically expresses problem behavior with greater intensity or duration than the "normal" child. The temper tantrum of a normal child may involve crying, stomping feet, throwing a toy, or slamming a door, and lasts five or ten minutes. The temper tantrum of the SLD child, however, may involve screaming, assaulting the adult, or breaking various objects, and last for a half hour or more. And when it's over, both the child and the adult are exhausted.

Third, the behavior of many SLD children is in some respects characteristic of "normal" children at younger ages. It is not unusual for a normal three- or four-year-old child to have a temper tantrum. When the child is this young, most parents survive the incident fairly well and do not become overly upset or anxious. If more frequent and intense tantrums occur with a child who is eight, ten, or twelve years old, it is quite a different story. The more slowly an SLD child matures, the more his behavior will deviate from that of peers and seem "strange," and the more anxious parents and teachers become.

"Why Don't You Act Like Johnny?"

In response to an SLD child's poorly developed social behavior and manners, his parents may ask, "Why don't you act like your friend Johnny?" This is a question the child probably cannot answer, but which certainly deserves an answer. It reflects the parents' perplexity, their desire to provide an acceptable model for the child to emulate, and perhaps their hope that such a question will enable their child to recognize his behavior problems and to change his ways. Unfortunately, it will not work.

One reason why an SLD child does not act like others his age is because he may lack the skills necessary for self-control. These and other skills develop unevenly and frequently lag behind the levels of proficiency expected at various ages. Consequently, the child requires special management, guidance, and support to develop such skills. An SLD child may have immature speech or language patterns, be behind in reading and math, and not learn to ride a bicycle until three or four years beyond the expected age. Similarly, the child may have immature or poorly controlled behavior patterns. Behavioral goals and expectations for the SLD child should be compatible with the child's **developmental levels** rather than the child's chronological age. This can be an important first step toward reducing the frequency of problem behaviors and helping the child develop better behavioral control skills.

Behavior is determined not only by self-control skills, but also by other related skills, previous experiences, interests, needs, and current pressures or stress. Problems associated with these factors may not be outwardly evident and might be easily overlooked by a parent or teacher, unlike the visible limitations of a physically handicapped child for whom modified expectations are readily made.

Everybody, including the SLD child, must assume some responsibility for his behavior. The level of responsibility, however, must be compatible with each person's skill levels and tolerance for coping with various amounts of stress.

Where It All Takes Place

Behavior is complex and has many interacting determinants. The better we understand these determinants, the more understandable the child's behavior becomes, and the more effectively we can deal with the child's behavior problems. For example, if a child's parents and teachers report that he "fights all the time," it is important to know where, when, and with whom. Does he fight only in unsupervised play activities or in any type of situation? Does he fight more frequently in the afternoons and evenings when fatigued or at any time of the day? Does he fight primarily with peers, younger children, or adults? Even if his parents have tried to teach him not to fight, has he ever witnessed fights between them? Even if his teacher has admonished him for fighting, has he seen an approving grin on the teacher's face when he explained how he "beat up" the classroom bully on the playground?

Any plan of action that attempts to manage a child's behavior problems must consider the child's feelings and his reasons for the behavior. At the same time, the management plan must consider the feelings of others who are involved, including those of the parents and teachers. Too often, parents and teachers are made to feel guilty because of the ways they have allegedly "mishandled" a situation. Their responses may have contributed to some of the child's behavior problems; however, most parents and teachers probably do the very best they can to cope with these behavior problems. Parents and teachers often admit that they could benefit from guidance to improve the effectiveness of their child-rearing techniques. Unfortunately, they may be either blamed or misguided by various specialists or told that they should ignore the behavior because the child "will outgrow it." Neither extreme is really very helpful for parents, teachers, or anyone who is trying to manage the difficult behaviors of the SLD child.

Instead, parents and teachers must: (1) become aware of the child's developmental levels in various skill areas, (2) recognize the child's feelings and needs, (3) analyze the situation in which the behavior occurs, (4) recognize the feelings and needs of everyone involved, and then (5) develop a plan of action. The following discussion will focus upon these issues.

SUMMARY ITEMS: BASIC ORIENTATION

1. The SLD child may display emotional upsets more frequently and with greater intensity than most children. The child may behave in ways that characterize younger children.

2. Skill weaknesses that are not visibly evident limit the effectiveness of the SLD child's performance.

3. Understand the SLD child's developmental levels in various skill areas to guide program planning and the selection of behavior management techniques.

4. Become aware of environmental or situational factors that influence the SLD child's behavior in either positive or negative ways.

5. Show respect for the SLD child's feelings and needs. Be concerned for the feelings and needs of others who interact with the child.

6. No child shows all the characteristics of a specific learning disability; each has a unique set of symptoms. What controls one child's behavior may not work for another. What works for one child one time may not work for the same child the next time. Techniques for each child need to be considered on an individual basis.

OBSERVABLE BEHAVIOR, UNDERLYING REASONS

"He Drives Me Up a Wall!"

part one

Let's examine more closely some of the classic behavioral traits of SLD children. The case histories of these children frequently mention similar behavioral traits which can be used diagnostically to identify children with specific learning disabilities. A single child seldom demonstrates all of these traits, but they appear among SLD children in various combinations and with various degrees of intensity. The behavioral traits that characterize any particular child are commonly associated with that child's pattern of skill weaknesses.

Not all SLD children demonstrate behaviors that are difficult to manage. Their behavior may appear relatively "normal" and their problems essentially limited to certain academic, speech and language, or coordination tasks. The cause or severity of their specific learning disabilities may be such that behavioral controls are not significantly affected. Their emotional distress may not be expressed in disruptive ways. Nevertheless, the frustrations and disappointments these children experience as a result of their learning disabilities nearly always impair their self-confidence to some degree. For this reason, the basic principles of behavior management to be discussed in Part II are applicable essentially to

10

all children with specific learning disabilities. The manner and degree of application must be determined by each child's symptoms.

Keep in mind that behavior has many causes that interact inseparably with each other. Be cautious about trying to develop overly simplified explanations for behavior. Perhaps only a few of the more evident and influential causes of the child's behavior can be identified. Several different behaviors may even share the same causes. A behavior management plan that recognizes at least some of the underlying causes for the behavior is usually more effective than one that is arbitrary or based upon the adult's anger and guilt. Even though a child's behavior is caused by, or is a reaction to, his insufficiently developed or impaired skills, it must not be concluded that nothing can be done to change or control it. Neither pity nor helplessness is a proper response.

Parents and teachers frequently use similar expressions when talking about an SLD child. These expressions encapsulate clusters of related behavioral traits which the adults have had difficulty controlling in the child. The following discussion uses descriptive vignettes to illustrate these clusters of behavioral traits and presents explanations for these behaviors.

The Hyperactive Child

"He's Always on the Go!"

chapter two

OBSERVABLE BEHAVIOR:
HYPERACTIVITY,
IMPULSIVENESS, DISTRACTIBILITY

My son, Jack, is seven years old. I don't know where he gets his energy, but he's never still. Even when sitting down, he's moving—tapping his feet, squirming in his chair, picking at a loose thread on his pants, and tilting his chair back (which usually results in his landing sprawled out on the floor). All this activity begins early each day and continues until late at night.

Jack is usually up each morning before anybody else has even dared to think about getting up. But soon there's no need to think about getting up; I have to in self-defense. In a matter of minutes, Jack has the TV blasting and has awakened his younger brother and made him cry. The dog yelps because Jack stepped on its paw while trying to ride on its back, and he's calling me to fix his breakfast.

Jack does almost everything in double-time. He runs instead of walking. He knocks things over. He shovels his food in so fast he is usually finished eating before the rest of the family begins. Even when I'm talking to him, his attention wanders, and soon he has changed the subject or is distracted by something else.

His teacher tells me that Jack is much the same at school. He seldom finishes assignments because he is so busy minding everybody else's business. He is often out of his seat and just can't seem to sit still long enough to complete even a short assignment. Jack's attention has to be redirected frequently. His school work is generally done incorrectly and sloppily, even the things he knows how to do. He seems in such a hurry to finish a task that he starts before really understanding the directions and then proceeds incorrectly or makes careless mistakes. When working at his desk, he does not complete one task before needing to sharpen his pencil, play with his eraser, or trace his pencil along some scratches on his desk top. It's almost as though he is bubbling over with curiosity and needs to investigate everything he sees or hears. Yet somehow his curiosity doesn't carry him very far. His interest in one thing is quickly exhausted and he is moving on to something else.

Home is rather peaceful when Jack is at school. I dread seeing the clock roll around to the time for him to come home; it's like opening the door to a hurricane. I can work all day to clean the house, but five minutes after Jack arrives it looks as if I haven't cleaned for months. My husband is often irritated with me when he comes home from work and sees the house disorderly. He blames me for not doing my job and doesn't seem to understand that Jack has produced all the chaos. In my husband's eyes, Jack is just an all-American boy. This is certainly a source of friction around our house.

I look forward to sunny days when Jack can play outside. Rainy days . . . well, forget it. It's like I'm a full-time supervisor. If Jack is noisy, I ask him to be quiet. If he's playing quietly, I must keep checking to make sure he isn't into something he shouldn't be doing. It seems that I'm constantly on his back with, "Do this, don't do that, why don't you try playing with this, and be careful you don't break that." Soon he becomes irritable, I'm already at my wit's end, tempers flare, and a bad situation gets worse.

My husband and I try to let Jack do all the fun things that most kids enjoy, but Jack usually makes each situation miserable for all of us. Last year we planned a big birthday party for him with all the neighborhood boys. It started off rather well, but soon he was so out of control that we had to end the party and send each boy home with a piece of cake. Going to parades or even a circus often results in a similar kind of turmoil. My husband and I end up feeling very embarrassed because of the way Jack acts in front of everybody.

And then there's bedtime. By this time I'm dragging but Jack is still going strong. He finds many excuses to delay going to bed. Once in bed, he's up a dozen times for water, to go to the bathroom, or to check a noise outside. If my husband has involved Jack in rough and tumble play just before bedtime, it takes Jack much longer to settle down enough to fall asleep.

As for me, I'm usually asleep before my head hits the pillow. I try not to think about what will be waiting for me when I wake up.

REASONS FOR HYPERACTIVITY, IMPULSIVENESS, DISTRACTIBILITY

It is normal for an infant's behavior to be extremely self-centered and determined exclusively by momentary needs. The infant's response is practically immediate to almost anything that satisfies the need for food, sleep, warmth, and security. The ability to wait for things to happen has not yet developed. For example, if the need for food is not met promptly, the infant does not conclude, "My mother is busy in the kitchen preparing the dinner for our family, so I'll just lie here quietly and watch the mobile on my crib until she has the time to feed me." Instead the demand for food is made clearly evident by crying and, if that doesn't work, screaming. This continues either until food arrives or exhaustion sets in, and the infant drops off to sleep momentarily.

As the infant grows, develops, and moves into childhood, this self-centered and impulsive behavior decreases. With the emergence of more advanced skills, the child becomes increasingly aware of the needs of others and better able to tolerate unmet needs for longer periods of time and control or delay reactions. Such skills contribute to the development of the child's ability to reason and plan ahead. In turn, the child becomes less impulsive and disorganized and more reasonable and controlled.

Unfortunately, the hyperactive, impulsive, and distractible SLD child has not been able to develop these skills as quickly as most children.

Some of the reasons for this are discussed next. Though interrelated, these reasons will be discussed separately.

Limited Ability to Control Responses and Plan Ahead

The normal child gradually learns to monitor and delay his responses to situations and organize them into appropriate, adaptive behavior patterns. If an SLD child has not yet developed these skills as well as his peers, his behavior may resemble or even be more poorly controlled than that of a younger child.

As children get older, they are exposed to more complex situations and more demanding expectations from adults. An SLD child's skills may not enable him to handle these increasing pressures appropriately, and he may respond with poorly controlled behaviors. Even situations that are not particularly demanding but are highly stimulating (such as a circus) may increase the child's activity level and make it difficult for him to respond in a controlled manner.

The SLD child may also show immature judgment in various social situations. When each of us decides how to respond to situations, we take many factors into consideration: socially acceptable behaviors, the consequences of various behaviors, the needs we wish to satisfy, and so on. The SLD child may be unable to recognize and consider these factors before responding. As a result, his behavior may be socially inappropriate and may even prevent him from recognizing the potential dangers in certain situations (playing with matches, climbing to high places, running into the street).

Adults often fall into the trap of expecting normal behavior from the SLD child who presents a normal outward appearance. The child is generally unable to meet these age-appropriate expectations and may react with frustration, anger, and noncompliance. This reaction may appear on the surface to be "deliberately disruptive," but may not be as entirely willful as it appears.

Limited Ability to Respond Selectively to Stimuli

Most of us respond selectively to **stimuli** according to whatever seems relevant to our needs or activities. For example, when reading an interesting book we may become unaware of surrounding sounds, such as a ticking clock. When driving down a busy highway, our attention is focused on the traffic and we may ignore much of the scenic landscape. The SLD child may have trouble making these judgments and focusing his attention in this manner. When faced with many stimuli, he cannot selectively attend to some and selectively ignore others. As a result, the child may give all stimuli equal attention without any priorities. Imagine the confusion this could create for the child. Concentration on a task becomes very difficult because of frequent distractions by stimuli unrelated to that task.

All of us have experienced some of this confusion and pressure whenever we have had several demanding chores to complete before an imminent deadline. We may have felt pulled in several directions at once and unable to decide where to begin first. Perhaps this is similar to the feelings some SLD children live with much of the time.

Inequalities Among the Five Senses

We learn about the environment through our five senses of sight, hearing, touch, smell, and taste. Many people have a preference for one sense over another. Some people remember best the things they see, others the things they hear. This preference may be stronger for SLD children whose perceptual handicaps interfere with the effectiveness of one or more of these senses.

For example, an SLD child sees a pretty vase full of flowers on the coffee table and wants to investigate. His mother says, "No, don't touch!" but he is already heading for the table, grabs the flowers, and knocks over the vase. His mother is understandably irritated and says, "You heard what I said, but you deliberately disobeyed me!"

Perhaps the child "heard" his mother, and perhaps he could have inhibited his response and obeyed her command. On the other hand, it is conceivable that some SLD children may "hear" such a command, yet not be able to inhibit a response already set in motion by a visual stimulus. A visual stimulus (the vase) may be more influential in determining behavior than an auditory stimulus (verbal command). Similarly, the behavior of other SLD children may be determined more by what is heard than what is seen.

Some SLD children seem compelled to touch everything they see. In some cases, this may be the result of a visual perception problem. For example, in spite of normal **visual acuity**, some children may have difficulty perceiving depth or differentiating the edges of overlapping objects.

The "meaning" of a visual stimulus may need to be validated through the sense of touch. It is as if they don't really trust what they see until they are able to touch it.

Emotional Factors

Hyperactivity sometimes helps an SLD child drain off the tensions and frustrations from daily experiences. In a more intense way, this is comparable to the times when most of us have felt anxious about a situation and derived relief through pacing or physical activity.

Hyperactivity may also reflect the child's pressured efforts to understand daily experiences. This may be comparable to the reaction of a college student who tries to relieve anxiety before entering a final examination in a very difficult subject by quickly and randomly flipping through his notes to reassure himself that he understands the material. The better the child understands his experiences and anticipates the appropriate response, the more confident and secure the child feels.

Hyperactivity, impulsiveness, and distractibility may also cover up a child's feelings of sadness or dissatisfaction. It is as though the child must remain overly active or involved with external stimuli to avoid becoming aware of inner feelings of unhappiness. Also, by remaining minimally involved with a task or situation, the SLD child reduces the risk for potential failure or embarrassment. He learns that it is safer not to try to do well in a situation and fail than to try and still fail.

This discussion should provide some appreciation for the complexity of hyperactive, impulsive, and distractible behavior. To label a child "hyperactive" or "impulsive" does not really help us very much in knowing what to do about it. Once some of the underlying reasons for these behaviors are understood, however, corrective steps can be taken to manage or change the behaviors.

CHECKLIST TO IDENTIFY THE HYPERACTIVE, IMPULSIVE, DISTRACTIBLE SLD CHILD

Use the following checklist of behavioral characteristics as a guide to identify the hyperactive, impulsive, distractible SLD child. When using the checklist it is important to remember two things. First, most of the behaviors described in this book are normal at various stages of development. A particular behavior might be indicative of a specific learning disability only when the behavior is more intense than normal for the expected age or is notably evident beyond the expected age. Second, no SLD child will display all the characteristics of the condition. The pattern of characteristics varies from one SLD child to another.

With this in mind, complete the checklist. Rate the child's behavior for each item by determining the frequency with which each behavior occurs: 1 (always); 2 (often); 3 (sometimes); 4 (rarely); 5 (never). The ratings for this checklist and those in following chapters are not to be totaled into a composite score, which is then interpreted as "good" or "bad." Instead, consider each item separately. A rating of 1 (always) or 2 (often) on any item would suggest that the behavior described is sufficiently intense to deserve further assessment to determine if it may be indicative of a specific learning disability (or even some other type of problem). Items that are rated 3 (sometimes), 4 (rarely), or 5 (never) probably fall within the range of acceptable or age-appropriate behavior and may not be significant. If one or more items are rated 1 (always) or 2 (often), refer to the chapters in Section II.

Behavioral Characteristics	*Frequency*
1. Excessively restless or fidgety when sitting (squirms in chair; fingers are busy doing something).	1 2 3 4 5
2. Seems more active than peers (nearly constant movement of some type; pace of movements is rushed or double-time).	1 2 3 4 5
3. Excessively talkative (talks nonstop; tends to ramble).	1 2 3 4 5
4. Acts before thinking (rushes into doing things without considering the consequences).	1 2 3 4 5
5. Very demanding of attention from others and wants immediate gratification of needs (has difficulty waiting for things to happen; might rudely interrupt what others are doing; unable to work for long-term goals).	1 2 3 4 5
6. Poorly controlled expression of feelings (moods change quickly; feelings seem more intense than expected for the situation; becomes enraged rather than irritated, ecstatic rather than mildly joyful).	1 2 3 4 5

Behavioral Characteristics   *Frequency*

7. Short attention span (shifts attention
   quickly from one activity to another;
   limited involvement with tasks).   1 2 3 4 5

8. Seems overly aware of stimuli (unable to ignore irrelevant noises, actions of others, or
   objects).   1 2 3 4 5

9. Behavior is aimless, not goal-directed (comments or actions are easily sidetracked and
   the initial intent or purpose of the behavior
   is ignored or forgotten; haphazard approach
   to tasks).   1 2 3 4 5

10. Disturbed sleep patterns (difficulty falling
    asleep; early riser).   1 2 3 4 5

11. Makes careless errors (accuracy and quality
    of performance on tasks are impaired by
    hasty responses).   1 2 3 4 5

12. Needs constant adult direction or super-
    vision (behavior becomes increasingly un-
    acceptable without supervison; depends on
    adults for assistance).   1 2 3 4 5

SKILL WEAKNESSES THAT MAY PRODUCE HYPERACTIVE, IMPULSIVE, DISTRACTIBLE BEHAVIOR

1. Insufficient inner controls to delay and modulate the expression of impulses and emotional reactions (behavior seems driven or pressured; expresses feelings or needs immediately regardless of the situation).

2. Impaired understanding of **cause-effect relationships** (runs into the street to retrieve a ball without realizing that a car may be coming; will not share toys with a friend and then becomes upset when the friend no longer wants to play).

3. Limited foresight and organizational skills (has difficulty anticipating the sequential steps necessary to reach a goal or complete a task).

4. Impaired ability to maintain goal-directed behavior (unable to ignore irrelevant thoughts, background noises, or other students while working in class on a reading assignment or on other tasks).

5. Impaired ability to discriminate relevant from irrelevant stimuli (during a class discussion of current news events, an SLD child may mention some unrelated incident that happened at home that morning).

6. Emotional immaturity; limited tolerance for frustration (cries or be-

comes angry quickly; seems overly dependent; overreacts to disappointments or difficult tasks).

7. Insufficient adaptational skills (resists changes in routines or ways of
doing things; needs time to understand and accept new situations; cannot
handle many stimuli at one time; becomes overwhelmed in highly stimulating situations; visual or auditory perceptual problems may impair the
child's ability to understand and adapt to the environment).

The Poorly Coordinated Child

"He Doesn't Watch What He's Doing!"

chapter three

OBSERVABLE BEHAVIOR:
AWKWARD, CLUMSY, CARELESS

Steven is our ten-year-old son. He's a well-built and handsome guy, but the clumsiest kid on the block. All his life he has been that way. We had hoped things would improve as he got older, but so far they haven't. At first we thought he couldn't see too well. We had his eyes checked, but the doctor said that Steven has 20/20 vision. To watch him in action, though, you'd never know it. It must be that he just doesn't watch what he's doing.

Steven can't walk across a room without bumping into a piece of furniture. If we ask him to help clear the table or dry dishes, we can count on his breaking at least one glass. You'd think he had ten thumbs. When he tries to pour a glass of milk, he either overshoots the glass or doesn't stop pouring in time to avoid overflowing it. When reaching for something at the dinner table, it is not unusual for Steven to knock over his whole glass of milk, which really gets the meal off to a great start.

Last week Steven wanted to make a small shelf for his room.

We gave him as much help as he would accept, even to the point of drawing the pattern on a piece of wood. When he tried to saw the wood, however, he cut every place except on the line. And when it came time to nail the pieces together, you never saw so many bent nails and bruised fingers for such a small project.

At times we have to laugh at the way Steven bungles through things, but then there are other times when it's really rather sad. The neighborhood children have stopped inviting Steven to play on their baseball team. Nine times out of ten he can't catch a ball that's thrown to him, and he almost always strikes out when he tries to bat the ball. The other kids just don't want a born loser on their team. We can understand that, but it's very hard for Steven to accept.

Steven also has problems in other situations because he doesn't watch what he's doing. For example, he turns in sloppy papers and makes careless mistakes at school. The other day the teacher gave the class a mimeographed page of arithmetic problems to solve. He started out doing well, but by the time he got half-way down the page he was making many mistakes. He even skipped over one entire row of problems. His work is so sloppy we don't know how his teacher can correct it.

For the longest time we thought he never would learn to dress himself. He struggled persistently to learn how to button his shirt and tie his shoes. When he almost had a button pushed through the hole, his fingers would slip, the button would fall out, and he'd have to start all over again. Or he would painfully go through the motions for tying his shoes, but the bows were always loose and fell apart when he walked.

Fortunately, Steven has learned to dress himself and tie his shoes rather well now. Perhaps this should encourage us to expect him to overcome his clumsiness in other areas some day. It seems that the first step toward that goal, however, is to get him to watch what he's doing.

REASONS FOR AWKWARD, CLUMSY, CARELESS BEHAVIOR

It may appear that the kinds of behavior described above occur simply because the SLD child does not pay attention to whatever he is doing. At times this may be true, of course. We all have our moments of clumsiness. There are other reasons, however, which also contribute to the clumsy and seemingly careless behavior of some SLD children.

Coordination Skills

Some tasks primarily require dexterity and speed and depend upon the coordination of muscles in our hands and fingers. Other tasks mainly require strength and endurance and depend upon the coordination of muscles in our arms and legs. Most of our actions involve some combination of both kinds of coordination skills.

Coordination skills determine how well a child can button a shirt, tie shoes, use a pencil, climb stairs, run, hop, and skip. Some of these activities, such as using a pencil or climbing stairs, may be performed reasonably well if the child moves slowly or puts much deliberate effort into it. Unfortunately, this not only requires additional energy, but is not always possible in view of daily schedules and pressures. For example, the teacher cannot allow an SLD child to take an extra half-hour to copy work from the chalkboard or complete an examination. When having to move at a pace that keeps in step with the world, the coordination skills of some SLD children begin to fall apart. This is analogous to the experience of anyone who is learning to use a typewriter. When typing skills are not well-developed, the beginner can type fairly accurately at a slow pace. If the person attempts to type quickly, however, many errors result.

Sometimes adults conclude erroneously that because an SLD child performs a task well one time (for example, a neat school assignment that had few errors but required extra time to complete), he should be able to do as well every time. If the child does not routinely perform as well as on a previous occasion, it does not necessarily mean that he is deliberately careless. Perhaps the child cannot perform at the expected speed or sustain the effort required by a task. Or perhaps an emotional upset temporarily decreases the child's motivation to do well on a task.

Visual Perceptual Skills

Vision provides us with information concerning the accuracy of our movements. If we are walking across a room and see that we are getting too close to a piece of furniture, this visual information tells us that we must alter the direction of our walking to avoid a collision. If a familiar room is darkened, we can rely upon our memory of what the room looks like to guide us through (assuming that nobody has rearranged the furniture since the last time we saw the room). Similarly, our vision helps us reach for a dish at the dinner table without knocking over something else.

Imagine the difficulty you would have trying to guide your movements with inaccurate visual information. If the visual information were accurate, imagine your dilemma if you could not interpret what the information meant. It may seem inconceivable that such a situation could exist with someone who has clear vision, but this may be true for some SLD children.

For example, an SLD child may have difficulty judging distance and may not alter the direction of his movements sufficiently to miss bumping into an object. He may have difficulty judging the speed of a moving object and not move his hands quickly enough to catch a ball.

Visual information may also be distorted if the child has difficulty making judgments about an object in relation to its surroundings. Any object which catches our attention takes on particular characteristics in relation to its surroundings. By comparison, the object is perceived as closer or farther, bigger or smaller, duller or shinier, or rougher or smoother than surrounding objects. Some SLD children have difficulty making these judgments.

Our perception of any object will also be influenced by the distracting quality of surrounding objects. If while reaching for an object, the child's attention shifts to another object, his movements may be poorly guided and appear clumsy. If the child is working on a page full of arithmetic problems, it may be easier to sustain attention on problems on the top line than on those toward the center of the page where surrounding problems can be distracting. The more the child's attention shifts to adjacent numbers, the more he is apt to make errors.

An SLD child may also have difficulty remembering things that were seen. This difficulty prevents the child from walking through a darkened room without bumping into furniture. It also limits the child's ability to remember spelling words or other information learned primarily by means of vision. Another SLD child may have difficulty remembering the movements necessary to complete a task. Such a child, for example, will have problems learning to skip or tie shoes.

CHECKLIST TO IDENTIFY THE AWKWARD, CLUMSY, CARELESS SLD CHILD

Use the following checklist as a guide to identify the awkward, clumsy, and careless SLD child. Remember that problem behavior displayed by an SLD child might be considered normal if it occurred both less frequently and with less intensity, or if it occurred in a younger child. Also remember that no SLD child shows all the characteristics of the condition.

With this in mind, complete the following checklist. Rate the child's behavior for each item by determining the frequency with which it occurs: 1 (always); 2 (often); 3 (sometimes); 4 (rarely); 5 (never). If one or more items are rated 1 (always) or 2 (often), refer to the chapters in Part II.

Behavioral Characteristics	*Frequency*				
1. Bumps into objects when walking or running.	1	2	3	4	5
2. Has difficulty tying shoes and fastening buttons.	1	2	3	4	5
3. Has difficulty cutting food.	1	2	3	4	5
4. Has difficulty eating neatly without spilling things.	1	2	3	4	5
5. Unable to run or skip smoothly.	1	2	3	4	5
6. Seems clumsy in sports or recreational activities (such as catching or throwing a ball).	1	2	3	4	5
7. Seems awkward when working with puzzles, models, or projects requiring dexterity.	1	2	3	4	5
8. Performs tasks sloppily (such as schoolwork).	1	2	3	4	5
9. Makes more errors on worksheets with many items than on those with few items.	1	2	3	4	5

SKILL WEAKNESSES THAT MAY PRODUCE AWKWARD, CLUMSY, CARELESS BEHAVIOR

1. Impaired **gross motor** and **fine motor** skills (such as legs, arms, hands).

2. **Perceptual-motor integration** problems (inability to translate visual information into appropriate or effective movements, such as moving hands in time to catch a ball or pouring a glass of milk without overflowing it).

3. Poor memory for the sequence of movements required by a task (for example, tying shoes or skipping).

4. Visual perceptual problems (impaired ability to judge speed of a moving object, to perceive depth and distance, to differentiate an object from its surroundings).

The Inattentive Child
"She Never Listens!"

chapter four

OBSERVABLE BEHAVIOR: INATTENTIVENESS

If I tell Janice once, I have to tell her a dozen times to do something. You would think that by eight years of age any child would be able to follow directions and do what she's told, but not our Janice. I might ask her to go upstairs to change out of her school clothes, wash her hands before having a snack, and bring down my apron that's on my bed. A simple enough request, wouldn't you say? But what do I get? She may go upstairs after I ask three or four times and finally drag her away from the TV. Once upstairs, she may get as far as taking off her shoes or blouse before getting side-tracked with a toy. I holler up several more reminders, each one louder and angrier than the one before. After many minutes have passed (enough to have changed her clothes several times), she finally comes down for a snack, but has forgotten to wash her hands and bring my apron.

I send her back to complete those two small requests, and you can imagine what happens. I hear water running and running and running. I yell up again, but she can't hear me over the sound of the water. By this time I'm furious! Up the stairs I go, only to find her filling the bathtub and floating a toy boat. A bit more scolding and on-site supervision finally get her through washing her hands. I send her downstairs for a snack, then I get the apron because it's easier and quicker to do things myself.

This kind of behavior is typical of Janice. My husband and I think that it's because she just doesn't pay attention and listen to what we tell her. She always seems so forgetful and absentminded. Janice still can't say the alphabet or even the days of the week in the right order, in spite of all the times we've gone over it. It just doesn't make sense; we know she's smart because of other things she can do so well.

We also have to watch carefully how we say things to Janice because she takes everything so literally. For example, the other day she overheard me say to my husband that from all the cleaning I had done that day I was "dead tired." Janice started to cry. Finally, between sobs, she was able to say that she didn't want me to die. This sort of thing happens time and again because she just doesn't take things the way we mean them.

We're worried that her not listening carefully to what people say may delay progress in school or keep her from becoming responsible and dependable.

REASONS FOR INATTENTIVENESS

Unusual behavior sometimes seems "cute" when the child is young, but becomes an increasingly serious matter if it persists as the child grows older. Any child may misunderstand or not follow parents' requests, demands, and rules for various reasons. But when the behavior occurs on a frequent basis or continues even as the child gets older, there may be other reasons to explain this behavior aside from "not listening carefully."

Understanding and Responding to Sounds

Even with normal hearing, an SLD child may experience various problems with sounds. These problems occur in the complex process of perceiving, interpreting, and translating sounds into appropriate behavior.

If several sounds occur at the same time, paying attention to one and ignoring the others may be very difficult for the child. In the previous example, assume that while Janice was being told to change her clothes, wash her hands, and bring the apron, there were other sounds in the background, such as a TV program. Her attention may alternate, not necessarily deliberately, between listening to her mother and trying to follow what is happening on TV. Janice might also find that keeping her attention focused on a visual stimulus (such as the TV picture) is easier than on an auditory stimulus (such as her mother's voice).

Sometimes an SLD child cannot distinguish subtle differences between the sounds or syllables of words. If the child misunderstands some of the words being spoken to her, the meaning of the message will be distorted and confused. For example, Janice's mother might say, "Put your hat on your head before going outside." Janice might misperceive this as, "Put your cat on your bed before going outside." The child's response may reflect this distorted and confused interpretation.

Remembering What Was Heard

Most eight-year-old children could easily follow the request to change clothes, wash hands, and bring an apron. The SLD child, however, may have trouble remembering things she hears, especially in the correct order. Parts of the request may be forgotten, parts may be completed in the wrong order, or the child may become distracted before finishing the request.

Consider the complexity of requests from the child's point of view before concluding that the child is simply not paying attention. The process of changing clothes contains many steps, involves many skills, and may occur in a room that offers many distractions. Perhaps Janice in the example has trouble buttoning and unbuttoning, tying and untying, knowing frontwards from backwards, deciding which play clothes to wear, and ignoring favorite toys or records. If so, simply finishing the first step of her mother's three-step request may be more than should reasonably be expected of her without some type of help or supervision.

The Complex Meanings
of Words and Experiences

Some SLD children use words they have heard others use without fully understanding what they mean. They interpret the meaning of words in a very literal way and are unaware of the nuances of meanings determined by the situations in which the words are used (such as "foot" meaning part of a leg or "foot" meaning twelve inches). They may understand the specific or concrete meaning of a word, but not the generalized or abstract meaning (for example, "home" for some means a house, but for others may mean an apartment, tent, or igloo).

An SLD child may also have difficulty understanding various social situations and deciding how to respond appropriately. There are many nuances of meanings among social situations just as there are among words. A response that is appropriate for one situation may not be for another similar situation. A response that is acceptable in a situation at one time may not be acceptable in the same situation at another. The purpose or nature of a particular social situation is reflected in the conversation that takes place in that situation. For example, compare the types of conversations and behaviors that typically occur at the dinner table, in a science class, on the playground, and in a Sunday school class. Or compare dinner table conversations and behaviors during a holiday meal with those following the death of a family pet. If an SLD child has difficulty perceiving these nuances, then social conversation, social judgment, and social behavior will be impaired.

A child's perceptions of a particular situation may lead to certain kinds of behavior that would not be accepted by the parent or teacher. For this reason, it is not enough to tell the child to "behave" in the situation; instead, state specific guidelines to define acceptable behaviors explicitly. For example, suggest specific comments or topics of conversation that the child can use. Explain why some of the child's previous comments or behaviors in a similar situation were unacceptable. Tell the child what types of behavior are acceptable and what types are unacceptable.

CHECKLIST TO IDENTIFY
THE INATTENTIVE SLD CHILD

Use the following checklist as a guide to identify the SLD child with problems perceiving and interpreting sounds. Remember that problem behavior displayed by an SLD child might be considered normal if it occurred both less frequently and with less intensity or if it occurred in a younger child. Also remember that no SLD child shows all the characteristics of the condition.

Rate the child's behavior for each item in the following checklist by determining the frequency with which it occurs: 1 (always); 2 (often); 3 (sometimes); 4 (rarely); 5 (never). If one or more items are rated 1 (always) or 2 (often), refer to the chapters in Part II.

Behavioral Characteristics	*Frequency*				
1. Needs to have instructions repeated for tasks.	1	2	3	4	5
2. Has difficulty remembering instructions completely or in the correct order.	1	2	3	4	5
3. Misinterprets the meaning of words, conversations, or situations.	1	2	3	4	5
4. Makes irrelevant comments in various situations.	1	2	3	4	5
5. Seems confused or misunderstands what is happening in a situation involving much conversation.	1	2	3	4	5
6. Recalls factual information incompletely or incorrectly.	1	2	3	4	5
7. Is more responsive to what is seen than to what is heard.	1	2	3	4	5

SKILL WEAKNESSES THAT MAY PRODUCE INATTENTIVENESS

1. Impaired ability to perceive and interpret sounds correctly and to respond appropriately (for example, "Put your hat on your head" may be heard as "Put your cat on your bed").

2. Impaired memory for information that has been heard (for example, can't remember the months of the year).

3. Impaired ability to understand rapidly spoken messages (similar to the adult whose ability to understand conversation in a newly learned foreign language is improved if the words are not spoken too quickly).

4. Impaired ability to understand complex or long verbal messages (for example, lengthy explanations or the use of difficult words may confuse and distract the child so that the purpose of the explanation is lost).

5. Impaired ability to generalize because of concrete thinking (for example, if a child were told by his mother never to play in the street, he might think that she meant only their street and not every one).

6. Impaired ability to understand nuances of words or situations (for example, the child misuses words which reflect variations of feelings, such

as angry, jealous, and sad or misunderstands situations in which these words are used).

7. Impaired ability to pay attention to relevant sounds and ignore other stimuli occurring at the same time (for example, a child may be unable to listen to the teacher and ignore the behavior of another student or the noise of a siren outside).

8. Various skill weaknesses may limit the child's ability to carry out verbal instructions from an adult even when the instructions are understood (for example, poor coordination and attention span may prevent a child from neatly copying a long list of spelling words).

The Resistive Child

"Stubborn, Stubborn, Stubborn!"

chapter five

OBSERVABLE BEHAVIOR:
STUBBORN, RESISTIVE, PROVOCATIVE

Our son, Jimmy, will be nine years old next week. Unlike our other children who are usually pleasant, cooperative, and fun to be with, Jimmy has such a stubborn streak that it's really hell living with him. Each situation becomes a major confrontation. He thinks everything should be his way or no way. If we ask him to do a simple chore around the house, all we get is resistance. Sometimes his resistance is subtle and he just ignores whatever we ask him to do, like emptying the trash can. The more we push and insist, the more openly resistive he becomes. Other times Jimmy is blatantly stubborn and obnoxious, especially if we are having to correct him or set limits on something he is doing. He typical response is, "Make me!" It's almost as though he considers us his worst enemies and every interaction takes place on a battleground.

Jimmy seems to have no respect for us as his parents. He seldom shows any signs of affection. In fact, he's never been the kind of child who could be loved or cuddled, even as an infant. You should hear the profanity he uses when angry. After all we've done for him you'd think he would show us a little respect and gratitude.

If we try to stand our ground when he's being stubborn and resistive, the situation quickly goes from bad to worse. Soon we are all completely drained and enraged, and nothing constructive is accomplished. Other times we try to ignore what he does, make as few requests as possible, or plead with him to change his behavior. No matter what approach we try, nothing seems to work.

Jimmy can also be provocative in such subtle ways that he comes out of a chaotic situation looking like an innocent bystander. For example, he will slyly do things he knows will upset his little brother. When we step in to calm things down, Jimmy responds to his brother's accusations with, "I didn't do that!" Or he will direct his provocativeness onto us and do little things that seem too insignificant to mention. Over time, however, these things erode our patience like water dripping on a rock. We lose perspective and overreact to each little incident. Perhaps the most irritating part of Jimmy's behavior is that these things seem so terribly deliberate, like he's really out to get us.

Occasionally, Jimmy can be very pleasant. But we have learned to be suspicious of this because often he is trying to manipulate the situation for his own benefit and at our expense. If my husband and I don't keep each other informed about our interactions with him, Jimmy cleverly plays one of us against the other and comes out the winner.

We are almost constantly on guard and distrustful of whatever Jimmy does. Our household seems to revolve around his needs, behavior, and daily power struggles. Our resentment is evident in our irritability and short tempers. We can almost understand why he considers us the enemy. But, honestly, he has driven us to this point.

REASONS FOR STUBBORN, RESISTIVE, PROVOCATIVE BEHAVIOR

Parents, siblings, and teachers often dread having to face each day with a child who displays this kind of behavior. This behavior can be controlled or changed, however. Later we will look at how this might be done. For now, let's consider some of the factors that contribute to this behavior.

Limited Frustration Tolerance

Whenever we have not been successful in completing a task or achieving a goal, we are initially disappointed. If we persist with the task or goal, and if each attempt results in failure, our disappointment leads to frustration, and the frustration leads to irritability or anger. We probably will abandon our efforts or seek assistance if we continue to meet with failure. Usually we can appease our frustration and anger by reminding ourselves that we are really adequate, worthwhile individuals. This enables us to take that frustration in stride and tackle the next task or goal that awaits us.

The SLD child responds differently. There are probably very few substantial successes in the child's past. It is difficult for the child to feel proud, adequate, or worthwhile. As the child's capacity to absorb more failure becomes overburdened, he will avoid situations involving any risk of failure.

It is understandable why a child with these kinds of experiences feels criticized by a simple statement like, "Jimmy, clean up your room." To him, he has failed to live up to his parents' expectations for neatness. He may feel irritated over this implicit failure and respond with negativism. He has been successful previously at winning power struggles, even if the success was limited to getting his parents upset. Power struggles may begin to characterize the SLD child's way of relating to others, sometimes deliberately, sometimes not so deliberately. Even when deliberate, the behavior is understandable. This may be his only form of success, dubious as it may seem.

The Need to Test Limits

An SLD child may need to see how much he can get away with before somebody yells, "Stop!" or before parents and teachers become upset. But why such a need?

Some SLD children may be genuinely unable to interpret a social situation well enough to determine what is appropriate behavior and what is not. They need specific guidelines for their behavior, perhaps with reminders each time they face a situation they tend to mishandle. Adults may have similar needs if they visit a foreign country with different social customs.

Other SLD children may be able to demonstrate appropriate behavior up to a point, but not know when enough is enough. They need reminders when it is time to stop or to control the intensity of a certain kind of behavior. The behavior of some adults at cocktail parties must similarly be kept under the watchful eye of a spouse or friend.

Other SLD children may need to test limits deliberately to elicit a controlling response from the adult in the situation. This provides reassurance that the adult will be capable of helping them regain control should such help ever be needed. In other words, losing control of emotions or behavior is another type of failure situation. Many SLD children need to test the ability of adults to help them through such situations. Sometimes a child's inner controls are effective only so long as there is a visible reminder (the adult's presence) that enforceable limits exist. This is analogous to the situation in which an adult is speeding down a highway and suddenly slows down when a highway patrol car is sighted ahead.

This is a sample of the various reasons why many children test limits some of the time and why SLD children test limits much of the time.

Poor Self-Image

Because of many previous failures, the SLD child often becomes self-depreciating. The child feels little pride in his accomplishments, has little respect for his abilities, and has limited aspirations for the future. It is unpleasant for anyone to feel like this. One way to ease the emotional pain, however, is to project this disrespect onto others. In so doing, the SLD child develops a disrespect for parents, teachers, or others in authority positions, and shows little gratitude for the help received from them. The child's own needs are so intense that the help received from others may seem insignificant by comparison. The child also feels little gratitude for others whose values, expectations, demands, and rules constantly force him to face the frustrations imposed by his skill deficiencies.

It is difficult to show love and respect for others until a person can feel love and respect for himself. The SLD child's poor self-image contributes to his feelings of moodiness and irritability. At one moment the child may appear happy and at the next be in tears or in a rage over some seemingly inconsequential matter. Each emotional blowup is one more failure experience for the child. Such experiences cause his feelings of frustration, anger, and self-abasement to increase. The SLD child may desperately want adults to help him control these feelings or the situations that arouse them. Whenever another emotional upset occurs, however, the child may feel unsupported and abandoned by adults. In turn, he feels little gratitude for adults and responds with additional negativistic and stubborn behavior.

The Need for Independence

An SLD child may recognize and even accept that he still needs help from parents and other adults to get through certain daily activities or tasks. At the same time, the child may want to assume the responsibility for some activities or tasks without help from others. He may want to attempt previously difficult situations in order to develop a feeling of accomplishment and pride. Whenever upcoming events are reasonably predictable, the child may want to decide in advance which situations to attempt and which to avoid to prevent failure. Being dependent upon adults, however, can make the child feel helpless in controlling daily events. The child may become anxious if he feels misunderstood by adults, unprotected from failure situations, and unable to predict what may happen next.

This need for independence, to be boss, and to gain some control over scary situations may be the basis at times for the SLD child's stubborn, negativistic, and irritable behavior. Refusals to comply or the "you can't make me do it" attitude may reflect the child's way of gaining control over feelings and potential failures. While you may understand the child's wanting this feeling of security, you cannot live peacefully with the child as long as such an attitude exists. Some suggestions for avoiding these confrontations are discussed in Part II.

CHECKLIST TO IDENTIFY THE STUBBORN, RESISTIVE, AND PROVOCATIVE SLD CHILD

Use the following checklist as a guide to identify the stubborn, resistive, and provocative SLD child. Remember that many of the behaviors shown by an SLD child may occur normally at some ages with less intensity and in younger children. Also remember that no SLD child shows all the characteristics of the condition.

Rate the child's behavior for each item in the checklist by determining the frequency with which it occurs: 1 (always); 2 (often); 3 (sometimes; 4 (rarely); 5 (never). If one or more items are rated 1 (always) or 2 (often), refer to the chapters in Part II.

Behavioral Characteristics	*Frequency*

1. Is self-centered to an excessive degree (demanding; wants his or her own way; unable to share toys; seems selfish).   1 2 3 4 5

2. Engages in power struggles with adults (takes a firm stand to resist doing things that are requested; does not conform to classroom rules or procedures; will not stop disruptive behavior when asked by parents or teachers).   1 2 3 4 5

3. Shows little respect for others (says or does things that upset others; does not show empathy or sympathy for others).   1 2 3 4 5

4. Blames others and denies responsibility for things that happen (it's the parent's fault that the child did not get ready for school on time; it's the teacher's fault that the child has difficulty with a school task; it's the baseball pitcher's fault that the child struck out in a game).   1 2 3 4 5

5. Tries to influence others in order to avoid difficult tasks or situations (pretends to be sick to avoid going to school; changes the topic of conversation to avoid discussing a problem; finds reasons to prolong a pleasant activity to avoid other tasks).   1 2 3 4 5

REASONS FOR STUBBORN, RESISTIVE, PROVOCATIVE BEHAVIOR

1. Limited tolerance for frustration (cries easily if plans are changed; becomes angry if unable to have his own way; tears up school papers if the task is too difficult).

2. Poor self-image resulting from an excessive number of failure experiences (has little self-confidence; thinks he is "stupid").

3. Self-disrespect which is projected onto others (thinks parents or teachers are "stupid"; disobeys the rules or requests of parents and teachers).

4. Limited frequency of successful experiences due to various skill deficits (compensates for failure by being provocative; "I'm successful in making the teacher angry even though I'm unsuccessful in reading").

5. Limited ability to interpret vague or complex directions (needs clearly defined, specific behavioral limits; instead of saying, "Play outside

with the ball in a safe place," say, "Play with the ball in the backyard, not in the street").

6. Insufficiently developed judgment or internal controls over behavior (has difficulty determining what is "appropriate" or "acceptable" behavior; needs adults to help control behavior, even to the point of providing physical restraint to prevent the child from injuring self or others or damaging property).

7. Limited ability to regulate reactions to situations due to immature emotional controls (responds to a mildly unpleasant situation with a severe temper tantrum rather than with irritability or slight anger).

The Hypersensitive Child

"Little Things Get Her Upset"

chapter six

OBSERVABLE BEHAVIOR: HYPERSENSITIVITY AND FEELINGS OF WORTHLESSNESS

Although eight years old, our daughter Karen often acts as if she is only three or four. The smallest thing can bring her to tears or make her angry. One minute she can be enjoying herself and the next minute everything can fall apart. Usually nothing has occurred to cause her to change, at least nothing that we can determine.

Karen is overly sensitive. She blames herself for everything that goes wrong and seems to feel that she is just no good. We feel sorry for her and try to show that we are sympathetic, but that usually makes matters worse. If I happen to be in a bad mood one day or if my husband and I have an argument, Karen seems to think that she caused it and may go to her room and pout.

Karen can also be very lovable. In fact, she seems to want too much affection and praise. Often she goes out of her way to do things to receive praise or reassurance. If we don't happen to notice or if we have not given the response she is seeking, Karen will ask,

"Was that good?" or "Do you love me?" or "Am I a good girl?" Sometimes it is hard to be sincere with our praise because she seeks this response so often. After all, there are things that an eight-year-old should just do without needing recognition and praise. But not Karen. If she doesn't get the praise she wants and as often as she wants it, she feels convinced that nobody loves her.

Karen cannot handle change or disappointments very well either. If I tell her that we will go shopping and then something delays our going, she becomes angry, cries, and perhaps even has a tantrum. She also gets upset if I drive a different route to the shopping mall, or if she has a different place at the dinner table when we have company.

Karen tends to overreact to other kinds of situations as well. For example, if a toy comes apart it becomes a catastrophe. If she cuts her finger slightly you'd think it was the end of the world. Actually, Karen is excessively concerned about any kind of physical injury, no matter how insignificant. She even becomes very frightened in situations when she anticipates getting hurt. For this reason she won't let us teach her to swim, she still can't ride a bicycle, and she avoids play situations that she considers dangerous. We try so hard to be tolerant of this behavior, but we do get quite irritated by it at times.

Karen has very little stamina for a girl who looks as healthy as she does. Mornings usually aren't too bad, but by afternoon she starts to feel fatigued and irritable. By evening she's dragging, I'm dragging, she's irritable, I'm irritable, and both of us are ready for an early bedtime. My husband is also tired each evening from his own day at work and has little tolerance for additional irritation. Evening is a time when we all have to watch our tempers extra carefully.

REASONS FOR HYPERSENSITIVITY AND FEELINGS OF WORTHLESSNESS

Many SLD children are hypersensitive. They respond to relatively insignificant situations with hurt, anger, jealousy, and fear. The kinds of situations that cause these responses can frequently be determined by observing and interacting with the SLD child. There is much overlap between the reasons for hypersensitivity and the reasons for previously discussed problem behaviors. Some of these will be reexamined from a somewhat different vantage point.

Poor Self-Image

Personal possessions influence how we feel about ourselves. Our feelings of pride are enhanced by a new outfit of clothing or a new car. For this reason, personal possessions are particularly important to the SLD child with a poor self-image. The child may overreact with sadness or anger when he breaks a favorite toy or rips a favorite article of clothing. Toys, clothes, or other possessions become in a sense extensions of the child. The integrity of these objects influences how the child feels about his own integrity or adequacy. If a toy does not work properly, it is probably broken. Similarly, if a child's brain does not work properly (that is, if the child cannot learn things as quickly or as easily as peers can), then perhaps it too is broken. If the child feels broken, damaged, or no good, his sense of integrity or well-being may be enhanced by having intact possessions. But if one of these possessions becomes damaged, the child may feel that his own adequacy has been further damaged or decreased.

Similarly, some SLD children overreact to minor physical injuries. Their feelings of adequacy are often influenced as much by physical well-being as by the integrity of material possessions. An SLD child may also become upset from a minor physical injury because of insufficient understanding of the healing process. The child's immature, concrete reasoning may prevent him from realizing that injuries are not always serious and will heal in time.

The child with a poor self-image needs to know that others have compassion and understand his feelings. Knowing that parents or teachers understand is quite supportive and reassuring for the child. Be cautious, however, that this compassion does not come across to the child as pity or sympathy. The last thing an SLD child needs (or anybody else in a similar state of distress, for that matter) is pity. Being pitied can be disparaging, which only reinforces the child's poor self-image. Rather than making the child feel comforted and supported, the "you poor child" type of response may intensify the upset.

The Fear of Unexpected Events

As mentioned earlier, the SLD child feels secure in knowing that his world is predictable. The more the child can anticipate what will happen each day, the better prepared he can become to cope with the events (even if the child's manner of coping is to avoid certain events). The SLD child has difficulty coping with disappointment or frustration and often needs time to plan and organize a response to new situations. This gives him a feeling of control over the outcome of events and the occurrence of failure. The SLD child who is unprepared for a situation may be unable to maintain emotional control or accept changes in routine procedures.

For example, if we are able to save only a small amount of money each pay day, most of us would feel more secure to place the money in a savings account with a guaranteed interest rate rather than in a speculative stock investment. If we had unlimited financial resources, however, we would probably feel less anxiety if market fluctuations lowered the value of our stock investment. Similarly, the SLD child with limited skill resources will feel more comfortable in routine situations that guarantee success than in those that change suddenly and may call for more skills than he has.

Perceptual and Coordination Problems

An SLD child's fearful response to situations may be related to specific perceptual and coordination problems. The child may fear failure as well as injury if a situation requires skills he does not have. If coordination is awkward even with both feet on the ground, the child may be fearful of learning to ride a bicycle. If there is difficulty timing arm and leg movements in relation to a moving object, the child may fear catching a ball or stepping on an escalator.

To illustrate further, suppose the teacher announces at the beginning of the school day that a game of touch football is planned for noon recess. The SLD child who fears physical injury, who cannot catch a ball well, or who does not understand the game rules has time to decide how to handle this potential failure. The child may pretend to become ill with a headache or stomach-ache before recess to avoid the game. While pretending to be ill does not help the child learn how to handle new situations appropriately, it does enable him to save face with his peers and avoid embarrassment from playing the game poorly. The perceptive teacher can pick up on these cues by counseling the child, arranging with the child's parents to teach him these skills in the privacy of the family, or giving him a status position in the game by being scorekeeper.

On the other hand, if the teacher does not announce the game until recess begins, the SLD child may feel trapped and overwhelmed with fear. His reaction under such circumstances is likely to be poorly controlled and perhaps explosive, a failure situation causing him to lose face with peers and feel even less proud of himself.

Whenever an SLD child is fearful of a situation, try to recognize that the fear might be associated with a skill weakness, a fear of physical injury or failure, or some related problem. Making fun of the child, telling him not to be such a baby, or becoming impatient and irritated seldom produces positive results. Instead, it convinces the child that nobody really understands his problems and only intensifies the child's fear.

Fatigue

Remember how exhausted you felt after your first day on a new job? The pressure of learning a new situation and the desire to make a good impression contributed to your tension and fatigue. This is perhaps similar to what an SLD child experiences every day. Pressures to perform well, criticism from adults, learning new skills, and remembering old ones all contribute to the child's tension and fatigue. Some SLD children fatigue quickly under such pressures and require more rest than usual in order to control irritability.

Other SLD children, interestingly enough, become equally fatigued by these pressures but do not appear fatigued. Instead, they become increasingly hyperactive. It seems that as fatigue sets in, the child's behavioral controls weaken, and impulsive behavior increases. Even though these children do not appear fatigued, periods of rest may reduce their hyperactivity and irritability.

CHECKLIST TO IDENTIFY THE SLD CHILD WHO FEELS HYPERSENSITIVE AND WORTHLESS

Use the following checklist as a guide to identify the hypersensitive SLD child with feelings of worthlessness. Remember that problem behavior displayed by an SLD child might be considered normal if it occurred both less frequently and with less intensity or if it occurred in a younger child. Also remember that no SLD child shows all the characteristics of the condition.

Rate the child's behavior for each item in the checklist by determining the frequency with which it occurs: 1 (always); 2 (often); 3 (sometimes); 4 (rarely); 5 (never). If one or more items are rated 1 (always) or 2 (often), refer to the chapters in Part II.

Behavioral Characteristics	Frequency
1. Feelings and moods change quickly, often without an obvious reason (seems happy one moment and is crying the next).	1 2 3 4 5
2. Assumes too much of the blame for failures or situational problems (feels responsible for arguments between parents).	1 2 3 4 5
3. Needs an unusual amount of reassurance, praise, and acceptance (gives things to peers to "buy" friendships; wants frequent hugs or expressions of affection).	1 2 3 4 5
4. Unable to handle frustrations, disappointments, or abrupt changes in routine age-appropriately (cries or becomes angry and upset if things don't go as expected).	1 2 3 4 5
5. Overreacts to situations with irritability, anger, or sadness (emotional responses seem exaggerated compared to what is expected in a particular situation).	1 2 3 4 5
6. Is overly fearful of physical injury (over-reacts to small cuts; is timid to catch even a soft ball; seems fearful in different play activities).	1 2 3 4 5
7. Becomes fatigued quickly (seems to have little stamina; requires much rest).	1 2 3 4 5
8. Seems to lack self-confidence (very reluctant to attempt new challenges).	1 2 3 4 5
9. Refers to self in derogatory terms (considers self to be "no good" or a "retard").	1 2 3 4 5

REASONS FOR FEELINGS OF HYPERSENSITIVITY AND WORTHLESSNESS

1. Poor self-image and feelings of hurt pride (may perceive self as "damaged"; refers to self as "stupid"; lacks confidence; depends on others for help).

2. Being different is equated with being "bad" (child thinks that because he cannot read or perform certain skills well, he must be no good or "bad"; a poor memory is equated with being retarded).

3. Limited understanding of cause-effect relationships (for example, mother burns supper and becomes irritable, and child interprets mother's irritability to mean that she dislikes him).

4. Extra effort is needed to compensate for skill weaknesses (painstaking effort is required if the poorly coordinated child tries to write neatly, for example).

5. Insufficiently developed inner controls over feelings (child is unable to delay or modulate feelings; responds to a situation with a violent temper when only irritability would normally be expected).

6. Many previous experiences of failure, criticism, and pressures to achieve (failures are not offset by a sufficient number of successes for the child to feel pride; child reacts to each frustration as others might react after many frustrating experiences).

The Self-Centered Child

"He Takes Every Ounce of My Patience and Energy"

chapter seven

OBSERVABLE BEHAVIOR: DEMANDINGNESS, PERSEVERATION, IMMATURITY

Our David is five years old and will be starting kindergarten next fall. He's a handsome little boy, very talkative, and really quite a charmer when he tries. His grandparents think the sun rises and sets around him. My husband tends to agree with them, of course, but he's away at work all day. He doesn't have to live with David day in and day out on a full-time basis.

In a way, you might compare David to those vacation spots that are considered "a great place to visit but you wouldn't want to live there!" People who are with David for brief periods of time are impressed by his verbal abilities and outgoing personality. They even consider him to be quite entertaining. Well, this is one kind of entertainment I can do without. David takes every ounce of my patience and energy. I'm counting the days until he starts kindergarten because then I'll be able to have some time for myself away from him. Perhaps I'll even begin to enjoy David more myself at that point.

Whenever I talk about this with my mother, she says I'm exaggerating. Actually, when I mention what David does, each thing really doesn't sound as terrible as I feel it is. Perhaps you just have to be there to appreciate what I go through. Let me describe some of the things he does that are so annoying.

First of all, he seems to have an endless supply of needs. From morning until night it's Mommy, do this; Mommy, do that; Mommy, help me with this; and Mommy, I want that. Or Mommy, why this or why that? Really, it's endless! Sometimes I try to meet his requests immediately, hoping that he will be satisfied for a while so that I can get some housework finished. But soon there's another request, question, or plea for help. Other times I try ignoring him until I finish whatever I'm doing, but that only makes matters worse. When I talk with my neighbors about this, they claim that their children do the same thing. It doesn't seem to bother them, however, like it bothers me. Maybe David just does these things more than most kids.

Another thing that really irritates me is his asking the same question over and over, even though I've answered it for him time and again. Or he'll repeatedly do something that I've asked him not to do. In one way or another, David needs to involve me in almost everything he does. I feel like my whole life is being controlled by him, which I really resent. I don't mean to sound selfish. After all, I realize that raising children can be a full-time job and that it involves sacrifices for parents. However, David seems to require more than I can continue to give.

Also, I don't trust David out of my sight for fear that he may get hurt. Other kids his age can play outside for periods of time without needing constant supervision. David, however, seems to have little appreciation for dangerous situations. He may run into the street to retrieve a ball without thinking to look for cars, or pull the dog's tail playfully and not realize that the dog may bite. Because of this, I must check on him frequently.

David's interests seem immature for his age. He actually seems to prefer playing with younger children than with others his age. If I think of him as being a couple of years younger than he is, his behavior and interests don't seem to be so unusual.

I guess it sounds as though I don't love David. That's certainly not true. I care for him very much, and I do feel guilty for becoming so impatient with him and for looking forward to his starting kindergarten. Yet, he has drained away so much of my energy and patience that I have little left to give.

REASONS FOR DEMANDINGNESS, PERSEVERATION, IMMATURITY

Living with an SLD child can be an exasperating experience, particularly for mothers and teachers who spend long periods of time with the child. The draining effects of the child's constantly demanding behaviors may not be as evident after a brief encounter as after several hours or all day. A parent's or teacher's love for the child can be quickly overshadowed with resentment. This reaction often becomes complicated by guilt and sadness for feeling resentful. In turn, the adult may compensate by being overly patient, loving, and helpful with the child. Such a reaction seldom improves the child's behavior and may intensify the adult's resentment because the child "doesn't seem to appreciate" the adult's efforts.

Let's look at a few of the reasons for this kind of behavior. Again, keep in mind that behavior has many causes. Avoid trying to oversimplify explanations. The following reasons are only examples of some of the factors that may explain such behavior.

Anxiety Associated with Skill Weaknesses

To varying degrees, many of us are aware of our strengths and weaknesses. We may become tense or anxious in situations that demand our weaker skills. To help us through these anxiety-provoking situations, we may seek reassurance and assistance from someone who can help us. Many SLD children also seek reassurance and assistance, but to a greater degree than most children because of their skill weaknesses. Some SLD children lack the confidence to function independently in practically any situation because their skill weaknesses are so extensive.

Frequently SLD children are overly reluctant to give up the dependent relationship they have with their parents or teachers. They may become very demanding and even seek help from adults for tasks they are capable of doing alone. They may fear making a mistake, being criticized if they do not perform well, losing control of their behavior if an adult is not present, or having to share the time an adult spends with others (another adult, sibling, classmate).

If asked why they behave in these ways, many SLD children could not explain. They may not even appear tense, anxious, or jealous when observed interacting with others. The feelings that motivate behavior are not always evident from observation. For this reason, a child may feel tense but appear relatively content. If you are not aware of the child's distress, but only of your own exasperation with the child, you may react with limited patience. When you understand the child's problems and feelings, it becomes easier to respond with greater patience.

Learning to Wait Is Not Always Easy

Infants are normally impatient and demand to have their various needs, such as hunger, met immediately. With maturation and experience they slowly learn to be patient and extend the length of time they can wait. They remember previous times when someone (usually mother) came to help them with their needs. This enables them to develop a sense of well-being and trust that somebody out there will come to relieve whatever their needs may be. Also, as they learn to talk, walk, and do things for themselves, their dependency on others is decreased.

For various reasons, many SLD children have difficulty learning to be patient and independent. One SLD child, for example, may have difficulty seeing similarities between a previous situation and a present one. Even though the child's needs may have been met adequately in the past, he may react to each new situation as though it were the first. Unable to tolerate frustration or tension, the child may demand help from an adult in order to complete a task quicker and with less effort. Even if the child attempts to complete a task alone, he may still insist upon the adult's presence because of the reassurance that comes from having a potential source of help visibly available.

Another SLD child may have the skills to complete a task, but be unable to organize his efforts. This produces a haphazard approach to tasks, making the completion of each a rather laborious process. The child may lack confidence, be afraid of becoming independent, and want an adult present even in situations that could be handled well alone.

Learning to wait for help or for events to occur may also be difficult for the SLD child with a limited understanding of time. It would be meaningless to say, "I'll be there in five minutes," to the child who does not know the value of one number from another. The child has no way to judge the length of five minutes to know how long he must wait. Persistent demands from the child for the adult's help may result.

Perseverative Behavior

Sometimes an SLD child seems to get pleasure from performing a certain task over and over again or making a statement or asking a question repeatedly, even though the adult has made the indicated response or offered an answer.

One reason for these perseverative or repetitious behaviors may be that the child has trouble changing from one situation or task to another. The ability to stop one type of behavior and start another may not have developed sufficiently yet. The behavior becomes so fascinating that the child derives pleasure from the mere repetition of it. An analogous situation, which perhaps we have all experienced, is when a tune pops into our heads and we hum it over and over until someone asks sarcastically if we don't know any other songs.

Perseverative behavior may also occur if a child is attempting to develop a feeling of mastery over some experience. Most infants, upon discovering parts of their bodies, enjoy endless moments of play with their fingers and toes. At older ages, children often relive a situation through play which previously had aroused anxiety. They may "play doctor" to have control over the experience of getting a shot, for example. As adults, we often rehearse repeatedly in our minds an anxious moment we must face, such as applying for a job or giving a speech. Such mental rehearsals help prepare us, at least psychologically, to face the situation. For similar reasons, an SLD child may perseverate upon an activity or statement in order to gain a feeling of control over his skills and ability to handle situations successfully. **Perseveration** may even occur in situations that have already been adequately mastered because pleasure can be derived from repeating a successful experience.

Emotional Immaturity

Raising any child can be at times an exhausting, demanding experience, in spite of the pleasures that are also involved. In retrospect, children grow quickly from one developmental stage to the next. Each stage initially brings with it a certain novelty for parents. As a child's needs change, so do the responses required from the parents. As the novelty decreases, so does the parents' patience. But difficult behaviors can be endured because they are soon replaced by some new aspect of the child's development. Besides, the many pleasures associated with raising a child make it all worthwhile.

Raising an SLD child, however, is usually quite a different experience. The child may progress slowly from one developmental stage to the next. This means that the difficult behaviors that occur with each stage of development must be endured by the parents for a longer period of time, and the intensity of this difficult behavior is usually more extreme than it is for other children. Furthermore, the pleasurable moments that offset the difficulties of raising most children may seldom occur when raising an SLD child.

The SLD child's development is generally uneven. Some skills develop approximately when expected; others remain undeveloped for longer periods of time. For example, an SLD child may have developed the normal coordination skills for his age. The same child, however, may not yet have developed good sportsmanship skills and is not accepted by peers to play on their teams. An SLD child frequently selects younger children to play with, because their skills are probably at similar or lower levels than his own. Under such conditions, the child can play and even compete with these children with little risk of failure. The child can leave a play situation with younger children feeling good about the experience, unlike the way he feels with same-age peers. The child's lack of normal skills can cause many unpleasant moments for the child, peers, and parents and teachers.

CHECKLIST TO IDENTIFY THE DEMANDING, PERSEVERATIVE, IMMATURE SLD CHILD

Use the following checklist as a guide to identify the demanding, perseverative, and immature SLD child. Remember that problem behavior displayed by an SLD child might be considered normal if it occurred both less frequently and with less intensity or if it occurred in a younger child. Also, no SLD child shows all the characteristics of the condition.

Rate the child's behavior for each item in the checklist by determining the frequency with which it occurs: 1 (always); 2 (often); 3 (sometimes); 4 (rarely); 5 (never). If one or more items are rated 1 (always) or 2 (often), refer to the chapters in Part II.

Behavioral Characteristics	*Frequency*
1. Requests considerable help from adults (wants parents to assist with dressing or to be a constant playmate; wants teacher to explain and help with each task).	1 2 3 4 5
2. Becomes easily upset in situations that require independent performance (may cry or become angry if adults don't respond immediately to requests for help).	1 2 3 4 5
3. Asks the same question repeatedly (for example, before going to the doctor for a check-up, the child asks several times, "Will I get a shot?" in spite of being assured to the contrary).	1 2 3 4 5
4. Performs the same activity repeatedly (spends much time stacking blocks and knocking them over; draws the same types of pictures over and over).	1 2 3 4 5
5. Shows poor judgment in social situations (has difficulty sharing or showing respect for the needs of others).	1 2 3 4 5
6. Acts younger than his or her age (social comments are naive; prefers play activities of a younger child).	1 2 3 4 5

REASONS FOR DEMANDING, PERSEVERATIVE, IMMATURE BEHAVIOR

1. Skill weaknesses and limited self-confidence arouse fear of failure (for example, the pain of previous failure with reading makes the child fearful of trying again without having the teacher help him step by step through each assignment).

2. Limited tolerance for frustration (child is impatient; feels an urgency to have each need met immediately; demands help from an adult).

3. Insufficient support skills (for example, although a child has adequate skills to write sentences, he needs the teacher's help to write a paragraph about summer vacation because he is unable to organize his ideas into the proper sequence).

4. Difficulty with transitions between activities (for example, the child may have difficulty changing the focus of his attention from reading to math or from recess to spelling; behavior appropriate for one activity may carry over into the next where it is inappropriate).

5. The need to master anxiety-provoking situations (for example, to gain control over a fear of dentists, a child may repeatedly "play dentist," either alone or with another child).

6. Limited understanding of social relationships and experiences (for example, because many of his skills are delayed in their development, a child relates to others in an immature way; although a 10-year-old boy can play baseball well, his immature social skills cause him to cry if he strikes out).

The Task-Avoidant Child

"If Only She Would Try Harder!"

chapter eight

OBSERVABLE BEHAVIOR:
AVOIDANCE OF TASKS
AND ERRATIC PERFORMANCE

For several years we've been trying to help our daughter, Pamela, do better in school. She's had trouble learning since her first day at school. At age twelve, she now has the attitude that she can't do anything well, so she doesn't seem to try anymore. Her teachers report that she never completes assignments and makes excuses for her lack of effort. If only she would try harder, we know she could do better.

Pam does some of her assignments quite well. We are convinced that she could do her other work just as well if she would just put her mind to it. She seems to understand whatever is being taught one day, but the next day she acts as though she never saw it before. In fact, sometimes she does better on difficult tasks than on easy ones. That wouldn't happen if she were trying to do her best.

To make her try harder, we take away special privileges, cut her allowance, and make her spend at least two hours studying every night. None of this seems to work. We all end up getting angry with each other, and her school grades remain low. We could understand why she doesn't learn well if she were not intelligent. The school psychologist has told us, however, that Pam has above average intelligence. Doesn't that prove that she just isn't trying hard enough?

REASONS FOR TASK AVOIDANCE AND ERRATIC PERFORMANCE

The motivation to do well influences how we perform in different situations. It is difficult to remain motivated, however, if our efforts usually result in failure as frequently happens with many SLD children. At times, insufficient motivation or effort may certainly explain their poor performance. There are also additional reasons why poor performance occurs on tasks that appear to be within a child's range of ability.

Fear of Failure

In the previous illustration, Pam may avoid a task out of fear that her efforts will result in another failure. Each failure produces increased feelings of inadequacy and insecurity. To say that Pam should try harder implies that her apparent lack of effort is always deliberate, and that to do better she need only decide to do so. The avoidance of tasks may sometimes occur without the child's awareness or because of feelings that are not easily controlled. Consider, for example, an adult who fears high places. We might use the straightforward approach of telling the adult that the fear is silly and to stop feeling that way. The adult's fear of high places will probably continue, however.

Remembering New Information

Sometimes an SLD child will be unable to understand the meaning of new information. Other times the child will be unable to relate new information to previously learned information. In order to learn such information, the child may rely upon **rote memory**. Unfortunately, information learned by rote is difficult to remember and apply to new situations in a useful way. The child may appear to understand rotely-learned information one day, but be unable to recall it the next.

For example, we might learn to recite an expression in an unfamiliar foreign language. Unless we can associate that material with something meaningful, we may have trouble recalling it the next day. Sometimes a new rule in grammar or a new procedure in mathematics may make as much sense to an SLD child as a foreign language. The task may be even less meaningful if the teacher presents the information verbally to an SLD child who has difficulty organizing and remembering things that are heard.

Recalling Previously Learned Information

Some SLD children, after learning something fairly well, are unable to retrieve that information immediately when it is needed on some later occasion. Strangely enough, the information a child is unable to recall on one occasion may sometimes be recalled correctly at a later time. For example, were you ever unable to recall someone's name and then remembered it after a moment of thinking or perhaps even the next day. The SLD child's difficulty with recalling information may be similar to this, but on a more frequent basis.

With the passing of time, all of us forget things we once knew. Those with better memories, of course, forget less than others. By reviewing previously learned information or practicing former skills, we can generally regain our earlier levels of competence in a relatively short time. Without review or practice, SLD children typically forget information or skills more quickly than their peers. They also tend to regain previous competence levels more slowly than others. This is particularly evident over long summer vacations. SLD children may forget more and recover it more slowly than their normal classmates.

What Skills Does a Task Require?

Successful performance on any task is dependent upon having the skills required for it. You cannot ride a bicycle unless you have sufficient coordination and balance. An average first grader cannot handle the homework assignments of a fourth grader. Because the skills of most SLD children develop unevenly, a twelve-year-old child may have a twelve-year-old's skills in some areas, a fourteen-year-old's skills in other areas, and an eight- or ten-year-old's skills in still other areas. If an SLD child can perform one task in an age-appropriate manner, it does not necessarily mean that all tasks appropriate for that age can be done equally well. The child's erratic or uneven functioning may reflect uneven skill levels, not motivational or effort levels.

CHECKLIST TO IDENTIFY
THE TASK-AVOIDANT,
ERRATIC SLD CHILD

Use the following checklist as a guide to identify the task-avoidant, erratic SLD child. Remember that problem behavior displayed by an SLD child might be considered normal if it occurred both less frequently and with less intensity, or if it occurred in a younger child. Also remember that no SLD child shows all the characteristics of the condition.

Rate the child's behavior for each item in the checklist by determining the frequency with which it occurs: 1 (always); 2 (often); 3 (sometimes); 4 (rarely); 5 (never). If one or more items are rated 1 (always) or 2 (often), refer to the chapters in Part II.

Behavioral Characteristics	*Frequency*
1. Seems disinterested in doing well on either school-related or other tasks (for example, the child's attitude is indifferent or even opposed to trying to improve performance in reading or sports).	1 2 3 4 5
2. Avoids starting or completing tasks (for example, the child's performance on a school task is delayed or interrupted by sharpening his pencil, asking questions, going to the bathroom, and getting a drink of water).	1 2 3 4 5
3. Offers excuses for avoiding or not completing tasks (for example, the child denies that homework was assigned or blames the teacher for not explaining the work sufficiently).	1 2 3 4 5
4. Performs inconsistently from task to task (for example, the child reads words well but cannot answer questions about what he read or cannot learn to spell the words well).	1 2 3 4 5
5. Performs inconsistently from day to day (for example, the child learns the months of the year one day but cannot repeat them the next day).	1 2 3 4 5
6. Needs more frequent practice than classmates to retain information or skills (for example, the child's reading skills decline notably from lack of use over summer vacation, whereas other classmates' skills may decline slightly or not at all).	1 2 3 4 5

REASONS FOR TASK-AVOIDANT,
ERRATIC PERFORMANCE

1. Poor self-image and hypersensitivity (for example, lacking confidence in his ability to learn, a child avoids doing homework; a child with poor reading skills causes a classroom disruption to avoid anticipated embarrassment in a reading group).

2. Limited motivation to achieve (for example, a child shows little interest in learning because his pride has been hurt so frequently by previous failures).

3. Delayed or impaired skills (for example, a fourth grade child can do arithmetic at that grade level but is reading at a second grade level because the skills necessary for reading have developed more slowly).

4. Impaired ability to recall information (for example, a child cannot think of a word he wants to use to express an idea; a child cannot immediately retrieve the answer to a teacher's question, but can remember the information when given time to think about it or when given a slight clue).

5. Impaired ability to retain newly acquired information or skills (for example, until new skills are well established, a child must have frequent practice to prevent excessive forgetting of the skills over long periods of disuse, such as over summer vacations).

The Optimistic View

"Don't Worry, He'll Outgrow It!"

chapter nine

A PARENT'S WISH

We've been concerned about Tom for three or four years. He was slow in learning to walk and talk, he seems immature for his age, and he's always been so hyperactive. Now he is six years old and has just started school. As we anticipated, we are already getting complaints from his teacher. He doesn't pay attention, doesn't do as he's told, and doesn't get along well with his classmates.

There are times when Tom can respond appropriately and be a very enjoyable youngster. These occasions are encouraging. They raise our hopes that he will develop normally and be able to live a happy life. When Tom was three years old we expressed our concerns about him to our pediatrician, but he reassured us that Tom would outgrow the problems. We really want to believe this, and we do feel hopeful as Tom learns to do new things.

When we see certain problems persisting, and even getting worse, we feel discouraged. We wonder if there isn't something that we should be doing to help Tom. Wherever we turn for help or advice, however, we get evasive answers and nothing is ever accom-

plished. With each complaint from his teacher, we keep hoping that someday perhaps he'll outgrow it as our pediatrician predicted.

A REALISTIC PERSPECTIVE

Parents naturally become worried whenever their preschool child does not attain the early developmental milestones at the expected ages. They wonder: "Are these important deviations from normal development?" "What causes my child to act this way?" "Is there something I should be doing to help my child develop normally?" These and similar questions reflect parents' concerns and anxieties and are often directed at the family physician or other professionals to whom parents look for sound advice and guidance.

Unfortunately, parents are too often told by the well-intentioned professional, "Don't worry, he'll outgrow it!" This type of reassurance is not only confusing for parents, but also very misleading. Does this mean that the parents should do nothing to help improve the situation? Does this mean that they worry excessively or needlessly about their child? Does this mean that when he "outgrows it" his functioning will be normal in every respect? Obviously, the answers will vary with the child.

Very rarely will an SLD child outgrow his problems with the mere passage of time. Unless appropriate help is sought, more often than not the problems go from bad to worse. Even if the problems are tolerable initially, they often become worse when the child reaches the age of nine or ten and enters fourth grade. By this time the curriculum in school has become increasingly abstract, relies more heavily upon independent functioning, and draws upon knowledge or skills that should have been learned in the earlier grades. Many SLD children who are chronologically old enough for fourth grade have not developed enough of the skills and knowledge necessary for successful performance at that grade level. Even if the learning or behavior problems were subtle enough to be explained away previously, the problems often intensify by fourth grade so that they can no longer be explained away convincingly. Usually the earlier a child's learning and behavioral problems can be identified, the better the chances that more significant problems can be prevented. Waiting until fourth grade to identify and help an SLD child may allow his learning and behavioral problems to become more intense and difficult to treat.

Parents and teachers may feel encouraged each time an SLD child responds well to a learning situation or behaves appropriately in a social situation. Specialized help is generally needed, however, in order to make those occasions occur with greater frequency and for longer duration. The specific nature of this specialized help will be discussed in Part II.

SOME BASIC QUESTIONS

● As a parent, are you frequently worried that your child is not learning or developing at the normal rate? For example, are the child's friends or younger siblings surpassing him in their skills?

● As a parent, do you think that there is nothing you can do to help your child with his learning or behavioral problems? For example, do you think of yourself as "just a parent" who must depend totally upon professionals for the help your child seems to need?

● As a parent or teacher, do you assume that because a child demonstrates good skills on some tasks, his problems with other tasks will eventually disappear without help? For example, if a child can repair a bicycle better than his friends, should his problems with reading be ignored?

● As a parent or teacher, do you conclude that a child must be retarded because he does not learn new skills as quickly as his classmates? For example, if a third grade child can read and do arithmetic only at a first grade level, must the conclusion necessarily be that the child is not as smart as his classmates?

● Has professional advice been of little value so far in helping you understand and deal with the child's problems? For example, have you been told to ignore the problems or have professionals disagreed significantly about what should be done?

If your answer to one or more of these questions is "yes," refer to Part II. The discussion in Part II should help to clarify these and other similar questions you may have.

Another Piece of the Puzzle

"Home, Sweet Home?"

chapter ten

Although everyone's behavior is affected to some degree by other people, situations, and experiences, the SLD child's hypersensitivity and tenuous emotional controls cause him to be affected to a greater degree. Carefully consider these influences when trying to understand and manage the SLD child's behavior. Only a few of these numerous influences can be considered in the scope of this discussion.

THE FAMILY AND COMMUNITY

Let's begin by looking at the composition of the family and surrounding community. Each family or community differs from another family or community in many ways. Also, a family or community at one point in time may differ significantly from the same family or community at another point in time.

The Family Composition

The SLD child's home environment will probably be emotionally supportive if the family is unified and harmonious, and if parents cooperatively share the responsibility for the child's care. If the family is in a state of turmoil, or if divorce or lack of cooperation places the responsibility primarily upon one parent, the home environment may be stressful for the child. When the responsibility for the SLD child falls primarily upon one parent, it is difficult to maintain an emotionally supportive environment. The drain on the parent's patience and energy becomes too great to tolerate without periodic relief and encouragement from someone else.

If the SLD child has no brothers or sisters, the home environment will be different than if parents' attention must be shared with other children. Sharing can be difficult for the SLD child. The child may feel jealous and resentful, especially as younger siblings develop the skills with which he is still struggling.

Older siblings may have sufficient skills and maturity to help with the care of the SLD child and lighten the parents' load. These siblings may also develop feelings of frustration and resentment as they experience what the parents have been going through.

Regardless of the SLD child's position in the family, more than a normal amount of sibling conflict is very likely to occur. Be sure to consider these conflicts when developing a plan for managing the child's behavior problems.

Community Resources

The community's sophistication concerning learning disabilities will affect the SLD child's development and progress. Neighbors may be tolerant of the SLD child's deviant, immature behavior patterns if they understand the nature of specific learning disabilities. They may even encourage their children to have patience and to include the SLD child in play activities. Unsophisticated neighbors, however, may not want the SLD child around their homes and may discourage their children from associating with him. Parents feel reassured knowing that their SLD child will be accepted by the neighbors and even helped or guided when necessary. On the other hand, parents feel apprehensive when anticipating complaints from neighbors or fearing that their child will be rejected whenever he attempts to socialize.

Similarly, the sophistication of public school teachers and administrators concerning specific learning disabilities plays a very important role in determining the course of the SLD child's development. The child's parents usually need guidance and advice about what a learning disability is and what can be done about it. These parents are fortunate if their child has a teacher who can identify the problem early, who can make the appropriate referrals for evaluations, and whose actions are supported by school administrators.

It is equally important to have sophisticated diagnosticians in the community who can further pinpoint the problem areas and recommend appropriate remedial programs or treatment. Unfortunately, parents are sometimes told by pediatricians that the SLD child will outgrow the problem, by teachers that the child is stubborn and lazy, and by psychologists or psychiatrists that the child just needs more love because of emotional problems. Parents become confused by these conflicting impressions. Whose recommendation should be followed? How can these professionals with conflicting opinions coordinate efforts to help the child? Under such conditions progress is delayed, the problem often becomes worse, and precious time is lost.

PERSONALITIES, ATTITUDES, EXPECTATIONS

The personalities of family members, teachers, and others who interact with an SLD child influence the outcome of each interaction. A calm, supportive, yet firm individual might enable the child to get through a difficult situation successfully. A high-strung, critical, indecisive individual might produce disastrous results. Similarly, a well-organized, systematic, and somewhat predictable individual might facilitate a more positive outcome than someone who is disorganized, impulsive, and capricious.

A person who is usually effective in working with a particular SLD child may not always be. A certain teacher may be able to manage an SLD child's behavior most of the time, but chaos may result on days when the same teacher is in a bad mood or the child feels too pressured.

The specific words used during interactions with an SLD child are considerably less important than the way they are spoken. Even though a parent or teacher says all the right words in a particular situation, the outcome may be unpleasant if the child detects an underlying attitude of criticism, impatience, or disinterest. Sometimes parents and teachers resort to punishment too quickly before considering how their approach to the child may have contributed to the problem.

It is sometimes very difficult to avoid feeling negative toward the SLD child. Brothers or sisters may resent the extra attention and consideration parents often give the child or feel embarrassed by the child's inappropriate behavior in front of their friends. Parents may respond critically because of the child's insufficient progress or resent the burden of raising a child with so many problems. Teachers may feel pressured by their full schedules and become impatient with the SLD child whose needs are taking too much of their time.

Finally, consider the expectations you have for the SLD child or that the child has for himself. An achievement-oriented family may expect more than is reasonable from their SLD child. The SLD child may feel obligated to set his goals too high in order to be accepted by high achieving family members. The teacher may know that an SLD child has average intelligence and expect faster progress than is possible in view of the child's skill weaknesses. In each case, a failure experience is likely to occur.

Once the child's skill weaknesses have been acknowledged, parents and teachers might set expectations that are too low or inconsistent. They might overly simplify tasks, withhold responsibilities, make excuses for the child's performance, or excessively protect the child from difficult situations. Having set low expectations for the child, adults may feel encouraged by the child's successful response and then present another task which is too difficult. Low or inconsistent expectations may limit the child's opportunities to develop new skills and prolong his dependency upon adults.

RELATIVES AND FRIENDS: A MIXED BLESSING

Parents of SLD children often need someone with whom to discuss their concerns. They need practical advice and a realistic perspective concerning the problems their child presents. Relatives and friends can sometimes meet this need. Unfortunately, well-intentioned advice is not always the most appropriate or constructive.

The advice may be pollyannish, denying that any problem exists. If perplexed parents develop a false sense of security by such advice, they may be delayed in seeking the necessary help for the child. Accepting the existence of a problem is the hardest first step to take. Nobody likes to admit that his or her child is less than perfect. Much time and energy are consumed as parents go through the stage of accepting false reassurance, developing excuses, and holding on to the empty hope that things will soon improve. Without help, the problems usually become more severe with the passage of time.

Relatives and friends may also exaggerate the seriousness of the situation by being overly critical of the child's performance and the parents' efforts. The anxiety this arouses in parents may either make them afraid to do anything or disorganize their efforts to help the child. Criticism can make parents even less effective than they may have been previously. As the SLD child becomes aware of parents' anxieties, the problems may intensify.

Fortunate parents have at least one relative or friend who can provide a realistic perspective, much needed support, and candid advice. This kind of guidance is beneficial for the SLD child, as well as the parents, if it leads to appropriate sources of help. When parents are ready to face the problem and take positive steps to correct it, their energies can be productively directed toward remedial help for the child.

PARENTS' FEELINGS AND PROBLEMS

It is normal for all parents to feel concern whenever one of their children has a problem of any kind. Depending upon the nature and severity of the problem, the parents' concern may develop into worry, anxiety, and fear about the child's welfare. Most problems that children have in the process of growing up tend to last a relatively short time. Parents feel relief as each problem is resolved. Whenever a problem persists for a long time, the parents' reservoir of energy may become drained to a critical degree. This produces the kind of fatigue that is not solved by a good night's sleep. Feelings of well-being, enjoyment of life, and optimism for the future are greatly decreased. Many parents of SLD children experience this intense depletion of energy and enthusiasm.

Parents of an SLD child may feel guilty that they may have caused their child's problems or that they are not doing enough to help their child overcome the problems. They may also feel angry towards each other because the problems persist. They may blame each other for mishandling the situation. They may resent the child's teachers because of apparently ineffective teaching methods or feel bitter about being burdened with an SLD child and become short-tempered whenever the child seems uncooperative. Sometimes parents do contribute to the problems, sometimes teachers do use inappropriate teaching methods, and sometimes the SLD child does not try to cooperate. These incidents represent only a portion of the overall problem, and something can be done to improve them. Some parents never go beyond the point of feeling resentful, angry, or depressed. They react to each issue by complaining or by feeling overwhelmed without attempting to use any corrective measures. This type of reaction can hardly improve the situation.

In some cases, a parent may have had similar learning problems as a child and may still have the problems as an adult. This might either enable the parent to have more understanding and empathy for the child or tempt the parent to overcome his or her own learning problems vicariously by demanding better performance from the child. Depending upon the way the parent responds, the SLD child may either benefit from the empathic support or be under increased pressure.

Often the SLD child must cope not only with his own inner problems, but also with these external pressures which result from the parents' problems and negative feelings. These negative feelings are very understandable in light of what parents go through in raising an SLD child. This situation can improve if parents alter their perceptions of the child and use more effective methods to manage the child's behavior. As the parents' interactions with their child improve, either through their own efforts or with professional help, the intensity of the child's behavior problems may decrease significantly. The suggestions and techniques discussed in Part II should prove helpful in effecting these improvements.

SUMMARY ITEMS

As you scrutinize and try to understand the child's behavior, avoid focusing your attention exclusively upon the child. Instead, view the child's behavior as a reflection of his interactions with the environment. Try to identify how different situations or reactions from others may be contributing significantly to some of the child's behavior problems. Making calculated changes in these situations or reactions may produce almost immediate improvement in some of the child's behavior problems.

Each of the items listed below might influence any child's behavior. When trying to determine the causes for an SLD child's behavior problems, consider to what extent these items may be contributing to the problems.

1. Stability and composition of the family: Are both parents living in the home? Does the SLD child have brothers or sisters? Do other relatives or friends live in the home? Does the family have established routines or predictable patterns of living? Are family interactions usually harmonious and supportive?

2. Achievement and competition among family members: Do family members set high goals or expectations for themselves? Does intense rivalry exist among some or all family members? Is achievement the primary determinant of self-respect?

3. The community's sophistication concerning specific learning disabilities: Do neighbors, teachers, school administrators, pediatricians, psychologists, or other professionals in the community seem to understand the needs of an SLD child? Do they know how to provide the help needed by an SLD child? Are they willing to provide it?

4. Personality traits and attitudes of family members and teachers: Which traits affect the SLD child positively? Which traits affect the SLD child negatively? Are family members and teachers empathic or aloof, patient or impatient, calm or pressured, discerning or rash? Are attitudes or feelings expressed directly or only indirectly through facial expression or tone of voice?

5. Personal problems of family members and teachers: How do family arguments or worries affect the SLD child's behavior? Does the child behave differently on days when the teacher has a headache or is in a bad mood? Does the child seem to act the worst on days when you have the least patience?

6. Appropriateness and consistency of adults' expectations for the child: Are expectations for the child reasonable or do they reflect the parents' and teachers' wishes for the child? Do expectations remain compatible with the child's skill levels? Do expectations change gradually or capriciously? Do parents and teachers share similar expectations for the child?

7. Support and guidance available to parents and teachers: Do parents have relatives or friends who can offer them emotional support and guide them realistically? Do teachers have other teachers or administrators who understand SLD children and can offer helpful suggestions? Are parents and teachers able to work compatibly on developing an appropriate program for the child?

PRINCIPLES OF BEHAVIOR MANAGEMENT

"Nothing I Do Seems to Work!"

part two

Coping with the behavior of SLD children can leave us feeling exasperated and perplexed. Parents and teachers often use one approach after another in their desperate attempts to keep these children's behavior under control.

A parent or teacher may rely upon essentially on-the-spot decisions with no substantial rationale for the methods used. Some adults are sufficiently intuitive to select effective and appropriate behavior management methods in this manner, but most will end up with methods that are inconsistent, ineffective, or even detrimental. The parent or teacher soon begins to think that nothing will work to control or manage the child's behavior.

Perhaps a parent or teacher may develop a very logical, carefully deliberated system. But the system may work well only occasionally or only when applied by certain adults. Parents and teachers may feel personally offended or inadequate whenever a technique does not consistently produce the desired results. In turn, they may switch erratically from one technique to another, searching in vain for a magical one that will be forever effective.

Between these two extremes are numerous other kinds of behavior management techniques that vary in effectiveness with each individual.

In spite of the technique used, parents and teachers are still left with many of the child's partially resolved or unmanageable behavior problems. The situation may eventually become intolerable.

No behavior management system can be totally effective. Even a computer, programmed to function in a specified way, may develop mechanical problems and produce undesired results. Generally we have only a portion of the information needed to predict, motivate, or modify behavior. However, enough is known about human nature to enable us to predict, motivate, and modify behavior to a significantly greater degree than would be possible if we were not to take this knowledge into consideration.

The more we know about the causes of behavior, the better we can understand it. The better we understand behavior, the easier it will be for us to select appropriate and successful methods for dealing with the behavior. The effectiveness of our techniques will be increased if we analyze and reanalyze our responses to problem behavior in order to learn from our mistakes. Do not expect success overnight. Change takes time. Some behaviors we may never be able to change successfully. Instead, we may have to compromise by finding the most effective way to contain the behavior or make it minimally disruptive to daily existence.

There is more than one way to manage each behavior problem effectively. The effective techniques are generally based upon similar principles of behavior management. Some of these principles will be considered in the discussion that follows. You can apply these principles immediately to daily management problems.

Recognize the Symptoms
"Where Should I Begin?"

chapter eleven

IDENTIFY THE CHILD'S
STRENGTHS AND WEAKNESSES

As a first step toward developing an effective system of behavior management for an SLD child, prepare a list of the child's strengths and weaknesses. Make a definite effort to be objective. Previous experiences with the child can bias your impressions.

Each parent and the child's teacher should prepare these lists independently. Later a comparison of the lists will reveal how much agreement exists between each parent's impression of the child as well as between parents' and teacher's impressions.

The following checklist itemizes typical symptoms associated with a specific learning disability. Through patient, systematic, and relatively objective thought and observation, decide which items are characteristic of a particular child and which are not. Rate the child's behavior for each item in the checklist by determining the frequency with which it occurs: 1 (always); 2 (often); 3 (sometimes); 4 (rarely); 5 (never). Items which characterize the child "often" or "always" should be considered a weakness. Items which characterize the child "rarely" or "never" should be considered a strength. Make a list of these strengths and weaknesses. Do not rate the child on skill items too advanced for his chronological age. Some parents may need to consult with the child's physician or teacher to determine this.

CHECKLIST OF SKILL PROBLEMS

Developmental and Coordination Problems	*Frequency*
1. *Sleep patterns.* Has difficulty falling asleep, staying asleep, or awakening.	1 2 3 4 5
2. *Gross motor skills.* Seems awkward when doing age-appropriate tasks involving arms and legs, such as running, skipping, jumping, or riding a bicycle.	1 2 3 4 5
3. *Fine motor skills.* Seems awkward when doing age-appropriate tasks involving use of fingers, such as buttoning, tying shoes, or eating.	1 2 3 4 5
4. *Body awareness.* Is unable to name and locate parts of the body accurately, or tell left from right on self and others.	1 2 3 4 5

Perceptual Problems	
1. *Visual-motor skills.* Is awkward on age-appropriate tasks involving coordination of vision with movements of arms or legs, such as pencil-paper tasks, coloring, catching or kicking a ball, or descending stairs.	1 2 3 4 5
2. *Visual perception skills.* Writes letters and numbers backwards (confuses "b" and "d" or "p" and "q"); reverses position of letters in words ("dog" is read as "god" or "on" is read as "no"); has difficulty spacing and aligning written work on paper (letters or numbers vary in size; words run together; errors occur in arithmetic because ones and tens digits are not properly aligned).	1 2 3 4 5
3. *Auditory perception skills.* Unable to distinguish the sounds of letters (for example, the "b" sound from the "p" sound); unable to distinguish words that sound similar (for example, words that begin or end with the same sounds).	1 2 3 4 5

Conceptual Problems

Frequency

1. *Thought patterns.* Thoughts tend to be disorganized, off the topic, or repetitive on a particular topic. 1 2 3 4 5
2. *Abstract reasoning.* Has difficulty interpreting the meaning of abstract words; thinks in a concrete or literal manner; seems unable to understand shades of meaning. 1 2 3 4 5
3. *Judgment.* Shows poor judgment when responding to a social or dangerous situation. 1 2 3 4 5
4. *Decision-making skills.* Seems very indecisive or overwhelmed by too many choices. 1 2 3 4 5

Speech and Language Problems

1. *Articulation.* Mispronounces common words to a noticeable degree. 1 2 3 4 5
2. *Syntax.* Uses "baby talk," improper subject-verb agreement, or the incorrect order of words in sentences. 1 2 3 4 5
3. *Receptive/expressive language.* Has difficulty interpreting the meaning of conversations or verbal directions; has difficulty putting thoughts into words. 1 2 3 4 5

Impulse Control Problems

1. *Activity level.* Seems overly active, impulsive, restless, or driven. 1 2 3 4 5
2. *Social restraint.* Does or says things in public which are embarrassing to others. 1 2 3 4 5
3. *Tolerance for frustration.* Unable to accept disappointments, changes in routine, or daily irritations without becoming upset. 1 2 3 4 5
4. *Perseveration.* Actions or verbalizations are repetitive beyond the point of serving a useful purpose that is apparent to others. 1 2 3 4 5
5. *Mood stability.* Feelings or moods fluctuate quickly, often with no apparent cause; has tantrums or explosive reactions even in response to rather slight irritations. 1 2 3 4 5

Problems with Attention

1. *Focus of attention.* Has difficulty becoming involved with a task; attention is easily distracted. 1 2 3 4 5

Problems with Attention   *Frequency*

2. *Duration of attention.* Unable to stick with
   a task until it is finished or to concentrate
   for reasonable lengths of time, even though
   no external distractions are present.   1   2   3   4   5

3. *Organizational ability.* Unable to plan ahead
   or to plan unstructured or free times.   1   2   3   4   5

Memory Problems

1. *Visual memory.* Has difficulty recalling the
   details and sequence of things seen, such as
   the correct spelling of words, facts from a
   story, or details of an experience.   1   2   3   4   5

2. *Auditory memory.* Has difficulty recalling
   the details and sequence of things heard,
   such as instructions for a task or details from
   a story read by the teacher.   1   2   3   4   5

3. *Memory for movement patterns.* Has difficulty learning and remembering the movement patterns necessary to perform certain
   tasks, such as skipping or tying shoes.   1   2   3   4   5

Feelings of Inadequacy

1. *Self-image.* Thinks of self in negative, deroga-
   tory terms ("bad"; "ugly"; "retard"); has
   little self-confidence.   1   2   3   4   5

2. *Tolerance for criticism.* Is overly sensitive to
   criticism (such as teacher's corrections on
   schoolwork) and subjectively unpleasant
   events (such as parent's angry tone of voice). 1   2   3   4   5

3. *Relationships with peers.* Finds it difficult to
   share; provokes fights; is unable to play according to established rules.   1   2   3   4   5

4. *Relationships with adults.* Gets into power
   struggles with adults; tests the limits of a
   situation to see how much can be gotten
   away with; oppositional and resists following
   rules or requests from others.   1   2   3   4   5

Academic Deficits

1. *Basic skills.* Has insufficient prerequisite
   skills needed for learning symbolic, abstract material, such as auditory and visual
   discrimination skills or knowledge of spa-
   tial relationships.   1   2   3   4   5

Academic Deficits	*Frequency*
2. *Reading skills.* Functions below grade level expectations in reading.	1 2 3 4 5
3. *Spelling skills.* Functions below grade level expectations in spelling.	1 2 3 4 5
4. *Mathematics skills.* Functions below grade level expectations in math.	1 2 3 4 5

There may be several items on one parent's list that differ from those on the other parent's list. Discuss the reasons for selecting the items and attempt to resolve the differences in the lists. It is not necessary to make the lists identical. The items that differ between the parents' lists may reflect genuine differences in the parent-child relationships or in the parents' impressions of the child. Parents and teachers should have similar discussions to compare the child's strengths and weaknesses in the home situation with those evident in school.

This process of observations and discussion is very important, but should be kept informal and casual. The process must not cause the family-child or teacher-child interactions to become distant or void of warmth and spontaneity. The SLD child must not become a specimen that is analyzed and discussed intellectually. Instead, the process is intended to facilitate an understanding of the SLD child. This understanding should lead to a more supportive, corrective home and school environment.

IDENTIFY THE EASY AND DIFFICULT TASKS AND SITUATIONS

Next, identify the tasks or situations the child handles appropriately and inappropriately. Try to be as specific as possible. For example, rather than just listing "interactions with peers" as one kind of problem situation, specify the nature of the interactions or play situations. Does the child experience the same problems with one playmate as with a group of playmates, with younger children as with older children, within a structured activity as within an unstructured activity?

Does the child's difficulty with a particular task or situation occur consistently? If not, look for subtle variations between the well-handled and the poorly-handled experiences. For example, a child may have trouble handling unstructured play activities with peers only occasionally.

Perhaps the composition of the peer group, the specific type of play activity, the availability of adults to supervise, the degree of competition, the child's fatigue level, or other factors play a role in determining the child's reaction. This scrutinizing of situations also helps you differentiate reactions primarily due to skill deficits from those primarily due to motivational or attitudinal factors.

Does the child handle anticipated or surprise situations more effectively? Being forewarned or prepared for an upcoming event enables the child to plan a successful response or at least to ready himself psychologically. Too much advanced notice concerning an upcoming event, however, may have a negative influence on the child's behavior because of his limited understanding of time or limited patience to wait. For some events a five minute advanced notice may be sufficient, such as telling the child that in five minutes (or when the big hand reaches the 12) he must stop playing and get ready for supper. For other events an hour, a day or even a week may be necessary for an advanced notice, such as preparing the child to stay with a new sitter while the parents go out to dinner or preparing the child for an overnight stay in the hospital. Generally, the more complex or emotionally important the event is, the more advanced notice the child will require.

Does the child perform more successfully when unpressured by a time limit? Some SLD children organize and execute their responses to a situation slowly. Successful performance may result if sufficient time is available. Failure may result if time limits are less than needed because of the child's slow functioning or impaired skills. Other SLD children might handle a task or situation relatively well in the morning, but respond poorly to the same task or situation when fatigued in the afternoon or evening. For example, an SLD child may have the skills to dress himself for school, but his awkwardness with buttoning his shirt and tying his shoes may require a little extra time. If enough time is built into the morning schedule, he may be able to complete this task successfully. If not, his mother may be left with the task. The child might be able to persist with buttoning his shirt in the morning, but become very frustrated with buttoning his pajamas in the evening when he is tired.

When listing the easy and difficult tasks or situations, consider the specific type of experience as well as the subtle factors that vary from one time to the next. Developing these lists requires careful thought and effort. The time spent is usually worthwhile because a meaningful foundation is established for building an effective behavior management system.

Some of the tasks or situations that are frequently difficult for the SLD child are listed below. Expand this list with other tasks or situations based upon your experiences with the child.

PROBLEMATIC TASKS AND SITUATIONS

Self-Help Situations
- Dressing
- Eating
- Bathing and grooming
- Toileting
- Bedtimes
- Other (specify)

Social Interactions and Responsibilities
- Interactions with parents
- Interactions with adults (neighbors, teachers)
- Interactions with siblings
- Interactions with peers
- Performing chores and other responsibilities (making bed, setting table, feeding pets)
- Other (specify)

Recreational Situations
- Entertaining oneself
- Arts and crafts activities (cutting, coloring, pasting, models, projects)
- Games and sports activities (table games, throwing and catching a ball, competitive sports)
- Special events (parties, movies, circus, holidays)
- Other (specify)

Educational Situations
- Reading-related activities
- Mathematics-related activities
- Other instructional areas (other academic subjects, physical education, industrial arts, music, art)
- Instructional input (independent seat work, individual instruction, group instruction, group discussion)
- Other (specify)

IDENTIFY THE SKILLS REQUIRED
BY EACH TASK AND SITUATION

As the third step, analyze the easy and difficult tasks and situations to determine the skills the child needs to perform successfully. By doing this, it should become evident that each task or situation is more complex than might be assumed at first glance.

Every task or situation involves several primary and supportive skills. For example, a seemingly simple task like getting dressed involves: (1) *abstract reasoning* to decide which is the top, bottom, front, and back of each article of clothing; (2) *gross motor skills* and *planning* to put on each article of clothing and in the proper order (underwear before pants, socks before shoes); (3) *visual perception skills* to distinguish right from left shoe; (4) *fine motor skills* to button buttons, zip zippers, tie shoes; (5) *judgment* to coordinate colors and make appropriate selections for weather conditions; (6) *concentration* and *attention* to avoid becoming distracted before finished; and (7) a *tolerance for criticism* to risk potential criticism from parents for taking too long or not having shirt tucked in properly.

You need not itemize every possible skill associated with successful performance on every task or in every situation. It is important to itemize enough skills, however, so that patterns of strengths and weaknesses begin to emerge. Note that similar weaknesses appear repeatedly for tasks or situations handled with difficulty, whereas similar strengths appear for those handled with relative ease. Sometimes apparent weaknesses will be associated with tasks or situations that are performed well. This might occur whenever a sufficient number of strengths are also involved to compensate for the weaknesses, or when the task or situation is presented with much **structure** to ensure successful performance. Similarly, an SLD child may perform poorly on a task in spite of having the essential skills. This can occur because of insufficient structure, distractions, low self-image, fear of failure, or a power struggle with the adult who imposed the task.

By the time you complete the three steps described above, you should have a fairly solid understanding of the skills and situations contributing to the child's failures and successes. Do not assume that this understanding guarantees accurate predictions of the child's future responses. There are too many variables that influence behavior for this to be possible. Nevertheless, this understanding of the child will enable you

(1) to exert considerable control over the outcome of daily events and (2) to provide the child with a significantly greater percentage of successful experiences.

EXAMINE YOUR OWN
THOUGHTS AND FEELINGS

The SLD child requires a disproportionate amount of time, patience, effort, and understanding from others. The primary responsibility for the child's care falls upon the parents, with possible assistance from other family members. This experience can be very demanding, draining, exasperating, and discouraging. Because of this, parents and siblings (and other relatives who may live in the household) may have many negative feelings and thoughts about the child in spite of their love for the child. These feelings and thoughts become an integral part of the child's environment. They must be considered when recognizing the symptoms of the child's learning disability.

"Why me?" the parents may ask. "What have I done to deserve this kind of burden?" Such questions are rhetorical, yet understandable. Parents dream of having the perfect baby (whatever that is) who will be lovable, intelligent, and capable of fine accomplishments. When the child turns out to have a learning disability with all the associated problems, however, a typical reaction from parents is: (1) to deny or excuse the emerging problems; (2) to feel depressed and guilty when it becomes obvious that the problems are real; (3) to blame one's spouse, the spouse's ancestors, or the obstetrician to relieve feelings of guilt; (4) to resent or even hate the child for having such persistent problems; and (5) to feel more guilt for hating the child. The child's environment and behavior will be significantly affected by how the parents express or resolve such feelings and thoughts.

Parents must try to distinguish their feelings for the child from feelings about the child's behavior. This distinction is hard to make when dealing with the behavior problems day after day. It is particularly hard when there is little apparent progress, and it seems as though the child is deliberately misbehaving. Parents begin to feel as though the child is out to get them. They may respond with deep dislike, if not hate, for the child.

At other times, parents may feel sympathy and deep concern for the child as he struggles to achieve and compete with peers, but ends up without success in tears. While the child needs support, understanding, and encouragement at such times, some parents are inclined to respond by becoming overprotective. Occasionally this overprotection stems from the parents' efforts to compensate for their own feelings of anger, resentment, or guilt.

These various feelings and reactions contribute significantly to the child's behavior management problems. Therefore, as a fourth step toward recognizing the symptoms of a child's learning disability, explore your own feelings about the disability, the child, and your expectations for the child. Through ongoing scrutiny of these reactions, you can gradually develop a more therapeutic (but not impersonal) attitude toward the child. Such an attitude goes a long way toward helping you come out with the "right response" at the "right time."

Similarly, siblings should explore their feelings and reactions to the SLD child. Depending upon the ages of the siblings, parents may need to help them recognize their feelings and find more appropriate ways to respond to the SLD child. Siblings must also be given their equal share of understanding and assured of their rightful place in the family. They often feel like second-rate citizens because of the special consideration bestowed upon the SLD child. Parents may even need to verbalize the siblings' feelings for them by making such statements as, "I imagine that sometimes you really get angry with your brother (or sister) because of all the problems that are caused by his (or her) learning disability." The siblings must also be helped to recognize and understand the SLD child's symptoms. Whenever something is understood, it is usually easier to tolerate. To tolerate, however, does not mean to consider the situation unchangeable. On the contrary, tolerant understanding contributes positively to the development of a therapeutic climate in which change is more likely to occur.

Teachers might also develop resentful and rejecting attitudes toward an SLD child. The teacher may feel frustrated because his or her busy schedule is disrupted by the child, threatened or angry because his or her authority is not respected, and helpless because he or she does not know how to deal with the child's behavior. Teachers, parents, and siblings may share many of the same negative feelings toward the SLD child, especially the child whose behavior problems complicate the learning problems.

THE REACTIONS OF OTHERS

After parents, siblings, and teachers have gone through this process of trying to recognize and understand the symptoms of the child's learning disability and their own reactions to it, the resulting insights may need to be shared with others. When appropriate, parents should share this information with relatives and neighbors. With guidance from parents, siblings may be able to pass along relevant pieces of such information to peers in the neighborhood. Teachers should inform other teachers or specialists who work with the child. Teachers might also share relevant information with the child's classmates in a way that will not betray confidence, but encourage greater acceptance by classmates.

This is more difficult than it may seem. Relatives, such as grandparents, may prefer to make excuses for the SLD child's behavior and problems. The grandparents may feel that their grandchild can do no wrong, and that the parents are overreacting. They may even recall that the child's parents did similar things when they were young. Neighbors may feel that the parents are trying to make excuses for the SLD child's unacceptable behavior, and that all the "spoiled" child needs is a good spanking. Teachers or administrators may feel that the child is just a "lazy learner," should try harder, or is emotionally disturbed. Peers may feel that the child is a "retard" or use the child as a convenient scapegoat for their own frustrations or feelings.

In response to such reactions, parents and teachers may be tempted to think that perhaps others are right after all. Be cautious about letting this happen. Usually parents, and especially mothers, are the first to recognize that something is wrong with their child. It may be difficult at first to be specific or even to put into words, but parents can often sense when their child's development is not progressing the way it should. Parents should allow themselves to be guided by these hunches. They should search for explanations and help until these hunches have either been confirmed or negated to their satisfaction. Teachers may have similar hunches after their efforts to tap the child's potential ability have been unsuccessful.

Keep trying to elicit the understanding and assistance of others. The coordinated help of all individuals who have important interactions with the SLD child is essential if progress is to be seen. Prior to the time when parents and teachers are able to recognize and understand the SLD child's needs, much random effort will go into their attempts to meet these needs. After they recognize and understand the child's needs, their efforts will be more appropriate, consistent, and effective.

Understand the Child's World

"I Never Thought of It That Way!"

chapter twelve

LEARN TO READ
THE CHILD'S BEHAVIOR

Our needs and wishes influence how we perceive ourselves and others, our daily experiences, and our environment. Problems, pleasant or upset feelings, aspirations, and fears influence our perceptions of situations and the ways we respond. We can not prevent this from happening. Each of us can recall times when we mishandled situations. Sometimes this happened even though the situations were not particularly difficult, but perhaps we felt depressed, physically ill, or under pressure from other demands. This happens in spite of our being relatively well-adjusted adults who meet daily responsibilities effectively and have our fair share of successful experiences.

If we have difficulty handling a situation well because of momentary discomfort or pressure, is it any wonder that SLD children have similar difficulties? Their discomfort or pressure is more than momentary. They have had few successful experiences to encourage them in times of stress. Their limitations prevent them from meeting normal expectations for their age. The better we understand the SLD child's complex problems, the better we can empathize with him whenever he mishandles a situation. This empathy enables us to "read" the child's behavior. We develop an awareness of how the child feels and why he responds as he does.

Avoid the "He Could Do Better If He Wanted To" Attitude

To assume that an SLD child is deliberately underachieving may cause parents or teachers to feel irritable and impatient with him. If the child actually has the skills to achieve at a higher, level, it may be necessary to find ways to motivate the child to do better. Does the child consider various tasks unimportant? Is the child fearful of another failure? Is underachievement the child's way of expressing feelings of anger toward the adult? By understanding how the child is perceiving a situation, you can respond in ways that are more constructive than irritability and impatience.

Avoid Reacting Too Quickly

Restrain the impulse to react immediately in opposition to the SLD child's maladaptive behavior. First try to determine what may be motivating or causing the behavior. Then try to satisfy the child's needs in ways that will encourage more adaptive behavior. Rather than saying, "He's doing that just because he wants attention!" or "He's just being stubborn!" explore the possible reasons why he may want attention or why he needs to be stubborn. Your response may be entirely different and more constructive once these possible reasons have been considered.

Avoid Offering False Reassurance

In an attempt to be encouraging and supportive, a teacher may tell a child that a particular task that is being avoided is really "easy." Suppose the child trusts the teacher, attempts the task, and fails. The experience of failure may be more intense if the child thinks he failed an "easy" task than had he been told that the task might be difficult, but that the teacher is available to help if necessary. Tasks that are considered easy by adults may not be easy for the child. A task that seemed easy for the child one day may be difficult the next if the child does not feel well, is worried about other things, or has actually forgotten how to do the task.

The more accurately you learn to understand the SLD child's perceptions of his world, the more empathic and supportive you can be. In all fairness, this is not "easy." What is easy, however, is to respond impulsively to the child's behavior on the basis of your own feelings or expectations. Your impulsive reactions may not be in accord with the child's needs and perceptions. It takes real effort to put aside your own feelings and expectations in order to focus on the child's perceptions. Even though you will make mistakes in judging the child's perceptions, the child will probably recognize your efforts to understand him. Don't be afraid to admit your mistakes to the child. A positive relationship with the child can be developed more readily through honest mistakes than through arbitrary self-righteousness.

A positive relationship between the SLD child and an adult facilitates effective behavior management. If the SLD child lacks sufficient behavioral controls to handle a situation appropriately alone, the child can often maintain more effective control over his feelings and behavior when he senses the understanding, encouragement, and support coming from the adult. A difficult situation is not as overwhelming when noncritical back-up help is readily available. Most of us enjoy receiving recognition for our efforts and acceptance by others who are important to us, and the SLD child is no exception. Whenever the child has sufficient controls to handle a situation appropriately, he is more apt to behave in ways that will earn him recognition and acceptance from adults with whom he has a positive relationship than to misbehave or deliberately anger those adults. On the other hand, if a negative relationship exists with an adult, the child is more apt to respond with rebellious, noncompliant, or passive-resistant behaviors. However, even when a positive relationship exists, support from the adult may at times be insufficient to help the child maintain control in situations that are perceived as too frightening, embarrassing, demanding, or unfair.

PROCEED FROM THE CHILD'S SKILL LEVELS

Develop expectations for the SLD child that are compatible with the child's present skill levels. These skill levels should be apparent after completing the procedure described in Chapter 11. Because many SLD children appear quite normal at first glance, parents and teachers often establish expectations on the basis of the child's chronological age. If the child is six years old, the adult may expect performance at the six-year level in every area. While some skills may be at that level, other skills may be at lower levels. Expectations must be adjusted accordingly. For example, a six-year-old child may demonstrate normal language skills, but have social skills at a preschool level. Such a youngster would be unable to handle successfully the typical play activities and social interactions of first grade children.

Learning usually takes place in baby steps, not giant ones. Similarly, expectations should be increased gradually as the child improves his skills. Concerned parents or teachers naturally want the SLD child to improve his learning and behavioral problems as quickly as possible. To accomplish this goal, they often increase the complexity of tasks too quickly, which almost guarantees failure. It is better to increase the expectations slowly and with small increments of difficulty. Be guided by the child's demonstrations of mastery, not by your desires.

DISCUSS PROBLEMS WITH THE CHILD

Sometimes parents try to protect their SLD child from becoming aware of his problems. They might even make excuses for the child's poor performance. This may partly reflect the parents' inability to face the problems themselves. Teachers might also gloss over problems or make excuses for the child.

Be assured that most SLD children are already painfully aware that something is wrong. They may not be able to explain what it is, but they recognize the discrepancies in their skills. Some tasks seem relatively easy, while others seem quite difficult and frustrating. SLD children also compare themselves with peers and siblings, and realize that they cannot do certain things as well as others.

Most of us become anxious when something unpleasant happens to us that we cannot control, or when we develop a physical illness that we do not understand. If the reason for an unpleasant situation is not known, we often imagine the worst. So it is with the SLD child. From past experience, the child knows that when a toy is broken, it will not work as it should. Similarly, if the child cannot learn as well as others, the child may think that he is also broken. The child may conclude that he is "a retard," "bad," or "no good." Something quite serious must be wrong if his parents avoid talking about it. Because most SLD children have some awareness of their problems and may exaggerate the seriousness of the situation, it is usually advisable to discuss their problems with them.

The content of such discussions will vary considerably from one child to the next. In each case, keep the discussions simple and brief, supportive and calm. Several sessions may be necessary to give the child an opportunity to think about the previous session and to ask questions as they occur. Use analogies that the child understands to illustrate the discussions and to liken the problems to something familiar.

For example, if you have an SLD son, tell him you have noticed how difficult it is for him to read (or do arithmetic, catch a ball, control his temper, or whatever). Indicate how very upsetting this must be for him. Nobody likes to have trouble learning to do things. Ask if he has noticed that most other kids his age don't seem to have this problem. Emphasize that just because he has difficulty learning some things does not mean that he is retarded or that such things will always be difficult. If he really were retarded, he would not be able to do such and such (mentioning specific areas of strength). Tell the child that it might be possible for him to learn to do things that other kids can do, even though it might take longer and require special teaching methods. Tell him that kids who cannot see or hear also learn some things slowly and need special teaching methods, but they are not necessarily retarded, just as he is not retarded.

Select analogies that are within the child's areas of interest. If the child is a sports enthusiast, he might be told that if a football player sprains his ankle, he won't be able to run as fast as the other players. That doesn't mean that the football player is retarded or "no good" in sports, but that he will need special help for his ankle. As his ankle gets better, he will eventually be able to perform as well as the other football players. Similarly, if the SLD child has trouble reading (or whatever), special help will be needed so that perhaps eventually he will be able to read as well as his friends. Remind the child about the things that were previously difficult but which are now done well (mentioning specific accomplishments regardless of how simple they may seem to the adult). In a similar way, the things that are now difficult may someday be easier.

These discussions must be at a level that the child can understand, in words within the child's vocabulary. Keep the discussion only as long as the child's attention span can tolerate. Several brief sessions may be considerably more effective than a single long one. Such discussions open the door for the child to ask questions about his learning disability. These discussions also let the child know that his parents understand, or that they are at least trying to understand, which may be just as important for the child. This provides the child with emotional support which may ease the pain the next time he is faced with a failure situation.

VERBALIZE THE CHILD'S UNVERBALIZED FEELINGS

As we face or anticipate various experiences in our daily lives, different feelings are aroused. At times these feelings may be difficult to control. If an experience is pleasant, we feel happy and excited; if unpleasant, we feel anxious, sad, fearful, or angry. These feelings may interfere with our ability to handle routine responsibilities. We become restless and unable to concentrate, and our thoughts vacillate between our responsibilities and the experience that aroused the feelings. We may feel the need to talk with others about our feelings and the experience, either to share our happiness or to relieve our sadness, fears, or anger. Talking somehow enables us to control these feelings more effectively, especially if we find a good listener who can really understand how we feel. Were we not to talk about our intense feelings with someone, we might become increasingly restless, spend more time thinking about the situation, and meet our responsibilities with decreasing efficiency.

Children, in general, have fewer controls over their feelings than most adults. SLD children have even fewer controls than their peers. For this reason, SLD children often overreact to experiences or respond with increased restlessness. Perhaps an SLD child lacks the skills to label feelings and put them into words. Perhaps the child cannot connect the feelings with the event that caused them. Perhaps the child has learned that increased activity decreases tensions, and never learned that talking can also decrease tensions. Perhaps the child has learned that talking about feelings or experiences is not rewarding because few people really understand how he feels.

For these reasons, the SLD child might develop better control over feelings and behavior if you help him recognize and verbalize the feelings being expressed behaviorally. Offer alternative methods for the child to use in coping with the situation the next time it occurs. For example, suppose that a ten-year-old boy feels jealous of his younger sister who can read better than he. Assume that he shows his jealousy through teasing, fighting, and arguing with his sister. When this kind of behavior occurs, the parents might say to their son:

> You must feel very upset because you are having to work so hard at school learning to read better. That's how I would feel if I were in your situation. You probably feel discouraged at times, too, even though you are making progress. I guess you've noticed that your sister doesn't have to struggle with reading like you do. I can understand how that could make you feel jealous of her and perhaps even angry. Maybe that's why you tease and fight with her so much. But you know, your sister can't play baseball or fix a bicycle as well as you can. Besides, Mommy and Daddy love both of you the same amount no matter what kinds of things are hard for either of you. The next time you feel angry with your sister, try talking with us about it instead of fighting. Fighting just makes everybody upset. If we work on it together, maybe we can find a better way to help you feel happier with yourself. Right now, I could use a big boy like you to help me fix supper.

Obviously, this example is overly simplified. The approach would need to be tailored to the situation and the child's needs. This type of discussion, however, can be effective in managing behavior. While it will not work for all SLD children, it does work for many. A one-shot statement will probably never work. If this type of approach is used consistently, it helps parents and teachers establish a positive, trusting relationship with the child. Trust is a basic ingredient in any effective behavior management system.

Usually it is best to wait until the child's behavior is under control before discussions of this type are attempted. A child is seldom receptive to clarification of feelings or interpretations of his behavior in the midst of a fight or tantrum. During such discussions, give examples of similar feelings or problems you have had, either as a child or an adult. This helps the child realize that adults are not perfect, and that perhaps it is still possible to grow up to be like Mommy or Daddy or that favorite teacher.

COMMUNICATE WITH MORE
THAN WORDS

Although many SLD children have difficulty with perceptual tasks, they can be extremely perceptive of the behavior and feelings of others. Their hypersensitivity and anticipation of failure and rejection make SLD children keenly aware of hidden messages that may be masked by very appropriate words.

Parents or teachers may select all the "right" words to help an SLD child with behavioral problems get through a difficult situation. If the adults are angered by the child's behavior, these "right" words may be spoken between clenched jaws, with a sarcastic tone of voice, or with a general body posture suggesting impatience and rejection.

At best, the child may receive mixed messages—positive words and negative body language—which can be very confusing. Which should he believe? The child may want to believe the words, but the body language and tone of voice are somehow more convincing. The child may respond to the nonverbal part of the message and ignore or not even "hear" the words. The implied rejection from the negative body language may cause the child to respond with even more intensified behavior problems.

Adults are frequently unaware of their negative body language. When dealing with the child day after day, their behavioral and verbal responses often become habitual and strained. They may not realize how the child perceives their responses. The same words communicate different messages to the child according to how they are spoken. Adults should become aware of their choice of words, tone of voice, and body language so that the intended message is communicated without making the child more confused or upset. When the words and body language send the same message, whether positive or negative, the message will at least be perceived as sincere. Sincere communications help establish a relationship of trust between the child and the adults, which greatly facilitates effective management of the child's difficult behavior.

ANTICIPATE PROBLEMS
RATHER THAN WAIT FOR THEM
TO HAPPEN

The wise adage, "An ounce of prevention is worth a pound of cure" readily applies to the behavior of SLD children. Once a power struggle has developed or a temper tantrum is full-blown, considerable time, effort, and patience are needed by parents or teachers to bring the situation back under control. The situation is made more complex if the adults react negatively to the child's behavior.

Behavior management is easier whenever you take steps to prevent or at least minimize the intensity of the child's problem behavior. This can be done by anticipating the situations which may cause the child to become upset. Either avoid those situations or provide the child with additional support to get through them successfully.

Present simplified and carefully selected experiences that can be handled by the child with a reasonable amount of success. Situations that must be avoided initially need not be avoided forever, but only until the child develops sufficient skills to handle them successfully. Such skills usually can be developed through a combination of the child's efforts, guidance and help from adults, and maturation. If potentially difficult situations can be avoided temporarily, or at least reduced in frequency or complexity, some of the behavioral problems that might otherwise occur will be eliminated.

For example, the child may become overly excited or upset in very stimulating situations with large crowds, such as a parade or circus. If so, avoid these situations temporarily. Select alternative forms of recreation or entertainment that are compatible with the child's skills and level of development. Having the child watch a parade or circus on television is less stimulating and more easily controlled by the adults than actually being present at the event.

It is neither possible or desirable to remove every source of frustration or irritation from the SLD child's environment. Exposure to frustrations and irritations in small doses may enable the child to learn gradually how to cope with such situations. By carefully observing the child, you can learn to "read" the child's behavior. The early signs of an emerging frustration, temper tantrum, or power struggle will become evident. For example, the child may show increased restlessness, impatience, or talkativeness or may become unusually quiet, moody, or disinterested. A certain body posture or facial expression may typically precede a major emotional outburst. As you become aware of these early signs and anticipate problem behavior, you can decide when and how to intervene. Sometimes it may be best to remove the child from the situation to prevent his becoming out of control. At other times, it may be best to move in supportively or with humor to help the child get through the situation successfully. At still other times, it may be best to ignore the situation (especially if you are being baited for a power struggle) or allow the child to handle the situation alone.

The appropriateness of your response will be determined primarily by your ability to "read" the child's behavior accurately. Sometimes this approach will not work well because you "misread" the child's behavior. Sometimes it will not work well because you moved in too late and the child's reaction was already well on its way to becoming a problem behavior. Sometimes it will not work for reasons that you may never be able to figure out. However, this approach can be effective often enough to make it a valuable technique for parents and teachers to develop.

DISTINGUISH BETWEEN THE BEHAVIOR AND THE CHILD

Try to sort out and label your many thoughts and feelings about the child and distinguish them from thoughts and feelings about the child's behavior. Do you dislike the child because of his misbehavior, or do you basically love the child but dislike the child's behavior? This crucial distinction influences your responses to the child, the child's responses to you, and the child's impressions of himself.

The SLD child generally feels inadequate, fearful of additional failure, jealous and resentful of others more fortunate, and confused by the perplexing demands of daily living. It is reassuring to the child to know that others are available to offer their support and assistance in difficult situations. Unfortunately, the SLD child's behavior frequently alienates others and drives away those whose help is needed most.

Reassure the SLD child that you will remain supportive because you care about him, even though you dislike his behavior sometimes. If the child feels hated by others, his ability to control behavior will be even less effective due to decreased pride and confidence. Think of your own response to stress situations. Can't you handle stress more effectively on days when you have a feeling of well-being than when you are depressed or dissatisfied?

After determining that it is the child's behavior and not the child that you dislike, share this self-revelation with him. The child's concrete reasoning limits his ability to differentiate self from behavior. "Bad behavior" may be equated with being a "bad person" or with being "no good." While it is especially important for younger SLD children to hear adults verbalize this distinction, older SLD children may also need or like to hear that adults can love them, if not their behavior.

If you have not yet clarified this distinction about the child for yourself, don't attempt to accomplish it during the middle of a power struggle with the child or while the child is having a tantrum. It will be nearly impossible to perceive such a distinction at those times. Instead, try to sort out your feelings about the child during moments of relative calm, such as when he is asleep or appropriately engaged in some task. Put yourself into the right frame of mind to consider this distinction by recalling fond memories or pleasurable moments you have had with the child.

It is extremely important to recognize this basic distinction between the child as a person and the child's behavior. Make a genuine effort.

SUMMARY SUGGESTIONS

1. Avoid the "he could do it if he wanted to" attitude. Because a child handles some situations as well as his peers does not mean that he has the skills to handle all situations that well. If an SLD child has the necessary skills to handle a situation better, motivate improved performance. A good first step is to become aware of the child's feelings and self-image.

2. Don't oppose the motives that are causing the child's maladaptive behaviors. Satisfy these motives in ways that will encourage adaptive behaviors. For example, a child may try to gain acceptance from his peers by becoming the class "clown" and doing things to make them laugh. The teacher can help the child earn his peers' respect and acceptance by acknowledging an area of skill or interest, by giving him a responsible role in a class project, or help the child in other ways realize that he can be accepted for his appropriate behavior more readily than for his inappropriate behavior.

3. Avoid offering false reassurance. Be honest with the child and back up his effort with your help and support. If you tell a child that a task is easy and he then has difficulty with it, his confidence in his skills and your judgment will decline. A more positive outcome can result if you tell the child that you will gladly help him if he finds the task too difficult.

4. Expectations for the child should be determined by the child's developmental levels, not chronological age. Increase levels of expectations and task difficulty gradually to ensure successful performance with mini-

mal frustration. A six-year-old girl whose attention span is similar to that of a four-year-old will probably not be able to finish many first grade tasks without becoming distracted. Briefer tasks may enable her to complete her work more successfully.

5. Discuss the child's learning or behavior problems with him in a calm, supportive manner. Present the problems in a realistic manner and offer reasonable solutions. Keep your comments specific and simple. Be willing to discuss these problems with the child on more than one occasion.

6. Verbalize and clarify the apparent feelings or motives behind the child's unacceptable behavior. Help the child become aware of the connections between his behavior, the reason for the behavior, and the effects of the behavior on others.

7. Avoid being the omnipotent, omniscient adult. Be ready to admit your mistakes to the child. Tell the child about frustrating or failure experiences you have had and how you handled them. If you lose control of your feelings with the child, be willing to discuss this when you regain control and explain to the child how you should have responded.

8. Monitor your body language to be sure that it communicates the same message to the child as your spoken words. If you tell a child that you will be glad to help him with a task, your frown and impatient tone may contradict your words. Sincere expressions of feelings, positive or negative, enable the child to develop trust in you which facilitates more effective behavior management.

9. Anticipate potential problems and take positive steps to prevent them. Help the child avoid failure situations, simplify the child's experiences, offer support and assistance to ensure the child's success, and keep a sense of humor.

10. Distinguish your feelings about the child as a person from your feelings about the child's behavior. The child needs acceptance and love even though his misbehavior may be very unacceptable and offensive. This does not mean you should smother the child with love whenever he misbehaves. It's all right to show the child that you feel angry when he misbehaves, but assure the child that you are angry because you dislike his behavior, not him.

Provide Structure

"Those Little Changes Make a Big Difference!"

chapter thirteen

DEFINITION AND PURPOSE
OF STRUCTURE

The term **structure** is used frequently in the field of special education. The term is used by teachers and other professionals in conferences with parents with the assumption that parents and professionals share the same meaning. Structure is an extremely important concept and must be understood by everyone who lives or works with SLD children. Perhaps an analogy will help to illustrate its meaning.

If one were going to construct a concrete patio, an essential first step would be to make a wooden framework to define the contour of the patio slab. Without such a framework, the moist concrete could not mold to the desired shape and would flow beyond the intended limits or contour of the patio. While the concrete is still soft, precautionary steps must be taken to ensure that environmental conditions are satisfactory so that the finished product is not damaged before it is ready to withstand external pressure. For example, it must be protected from the hot sun and kept sufficiently moist so that it dries properly without cracking. Also, people are kept off the moist concrete so that footprints or other imperfections are not left as permanent impressions. Once the concrete has hardened, however, the framework may be removed, and the patio will be able to retain its shape and withstand the pressures of daily use. If one wanted to enclose the patio, it would then be ready for the next step of the construction process.

Similarly, the SLD child needs a framework that defines limits and molds his growth and development so that the finished product approximates desirable patterns of behavior and achievement. The SLD child also needs to have precautionary steps taken to ensure that environmental conditions will maximize success and minimize excessive, premature pressure. As each step of a particular task or situation is satisfactorily completed, the child can be presented with the next step. As inner controls, emotional strength, and relevant skills increase, the child's need for external structure decreases, and he will be able to handle the pressures of daily living more successfully.

Structure can be defined as the calibrated, consistent use of appropriate guidance and support, specific limits and consequences, predetermined schedules and procedures, and simplified experiences to provide the SLD child with optimal success. The child's strengths and weaknesses relative to the skills required for successful performance in a particular situation determine the type and duration of structure to be used. Clearly, the use of structure must be prescriptive to the child's needs.

Children, in general, feel more secure whenever structure is fair and clearly defined than when it is arbitrary and vague. They need to know what kinds of behavior are acceptable in each situation and which activities they may engage in without direct supervision from an adult. Although they may not admit it, children usually feel reassured by the knowledge that adults will enforce structure because they care about them. This is especially true for SLD children. They often lack sufficient inner controls and other skills to manage their own behavior and handle age-appropriate tasks successfully. They must rely upon adults for help.

Structure is most effective when applied with empathy, firmness, and consistency. The child's needs should determine the type and duration of structure. Keep in mind that firmness is not the same as harshness. You can mean business without being rejecting, and be consistent as well as flexible. Structure may need to be adjusted to changes in circumstances or to each child's needs. By applying structure in a relatively consistent manner, adults provide the SLD child with supportive reassurance that the environment is somewhat predictable and stable. This helps the child anticipate routine events so that he can be better prepared to respond appropriately.

TYPES OF STRUCTURE

There are many variations of structure. These can be categorized under three basic types: task structure, situational structure, and relationship structure.

Task Structure

Present each task in a manner that ensures that the child (1) understands what needs to be done, (2) is not overwhelmed by the size or complexity of the task, (3) is given sufficient cues to minimize frustration, and (4) can successfully complete the task with a sense of accomplishment and pride. Frequently a task that seems simple and routine to parents and teachers may seem difficult to the child. This even includes tasks the child has been told or shown how to do on previous occasions. The degree of difficulty the child experiences with a task is determined partly by skill weaknesses and partly by the fear of another failure.

Depending upon the task and the child's level of development, use one or more of the following types of task structure:

1. Select tasks that are either well within the child's range of capabilities or only slightly more difficult than those that can be successfully performed independently.

2. Be sure to elicit the child's attention before explaining the task. Either establish eye contact with the child or focus the child's attention on the task.

3. Explain the instructions slowly, using simple words and short sentences. Patiently repeat the instructions if necessary.

4. Supplement verbal instructions with picture cues or actual demonstrations. When using demonstrations, proceed through each step slowly.

5. Break down complex tasks into sequential parts. Be sure that the child understands each part before presenting the next one.

6. Help the child actually move through the performance of a task if necessary. For example, when learning to draw different shapes, guide the child's hand (manually or with templates) through the movements that produce each shape.

7. Offer supportive reassurance whenever the child's attention or motivation begins to decrease.

8. Monitor the child's performance. With noncritical comments, guide his efforts toward successful completion of the task.

9. If the child is unsuccessful with a task, praise his effort and provide the opportunity to try again.

10. While repetition or practice is important, do not make excessive demands of the child at any one time.

11. Remember that there is more than one way to reach a goal. Most skills, such as various social or educational skills, may be taught in a variety of ways. Do not persist with a particular task or procedure if it always results in frustration, failure, or a power struggle. Be prepared to select alternate tasks or procedures that will develop the same skills but in a more harmonious way.

Achievement takes time. Although parents and teachers want the child to perform at higher levels as soon as possible, the process cannot be rushed. Too much pressure produces negative side effects, such as stubborn refusal to ever try again.

To illustrate task structure, suppose a young SLD girl were told by her mother to "get dressed for school." That may sound like a rather easy assignment, but there are actually many complicated steps involved in getting dressed. There are also many extraneous factors that could interfere, such as distractibility, not wanting to go to school, or being in a bad mood. In the process of getting dressed, the child must first select the appropriate articles of clothing (appropriate for weather conditions, color coordination, and size). The child must next put on each article of clothing in the proper order (underwear before skirt or slacks) and in the correct manner (front side of the clothing on the front side of the body, right shoe on the right foot).

To structure this task for the child, some or all of the following steps may be necessary: (1) pre-select the articles of clothing to be worn; (2) select clothing that the child can manage easily (for example, avoid clothing with small buttons); (3) stack the clothing in the order that each article is put on; (4) guide the child's efforts with verbal directions; and (5) give the child cues to help her learn the top, bottom, front, back, right, and left of each article of clothing. For example, mark an "X" on the inside of each shoe on the side next to the other shoe. When the shoes are placed side-by-side with the "X's" together, the right and left shoes will be in correct position.

Your goal is to help the child eventually learn to select appropriate clothing and get dressed without needing help from an adult. To reach this goal, present the structure in a manner that will be teaching the child these skills. Consider, for example, the suggestion of pre-selecting the clothing the child is going to wear the following day to school. In the child's presence, the mother might initially think out loud as she goes through each step of selecting the clothing ("Let's see, tomorrow is going to be very cold so you will want to wear warm slacks and a sweater. These grey slacks are warm and this blue sweater will look nice with them."). When the mother thinks the child is ready for the next step in the learning process (after several days or weeks, according to the child's rate of learning), she should help the child reason out the procedure for selecting clothes ("It's going to be very cold tomorrow. Which of your slacks would keep you warm? That's right, your grey slacks and your green slacks are the warmest. Now, which pair would you like to wear?"). In a similar manner, guide the child's thinking and performance in the other steps of getting dressed. Gradually reduce your input as the child learns to make the appropriate decisions and perform each step successfully.

To illustrate task structure further, consider the process of teaching an SLD boy to catch a ball. The teaching process must consider the child's skill problems and fears. Assume that the child's skills necessitate starting at a very basic level with much structure.

The teaching situation should be informal and relaxed, with the goal of having fun. Avoid too much of the "pay attention because now I'm going to teach you how to catch a ball" attitude. Allow the "teaching" session to last only as long as the child's interest and attention span will permit. Keep the experience pleasant. Perhaps only the child and the person helping him learn the skill should be present initially. An audience of any type may be too much stress because of potential embarrassment. Begin by tossing a large, colorful beach ball back and forth. The beach ball's size makes it easier to see than a baseball as it glides through the air and easier to catch. Besides being lighter than a baseball, it is also less likely to hurt the child if it hits his body instead of being caught. The distance between the child and adult should be determined by the child's ability to catch the ball. The distance might be ten feet or only one. Successful performance is the determining factor. As the child's skill develops, gradually increase the distance the ball is tossed. The number of play sessions needed until the child can catch the ball consistently over a distance of several feet depends upon the child's rate of learning.

When this is achieved (and please be patient), substitute a smaller rubber ball or a tether ball and start the process over again. The distance between the child and adult may need to be much less than it was at the final stages of catching the beach ball. Gradually increase the distance as skills improve. Give verbal cues to supplement the visual cues the child receives from watching the ball approach. For example, remind the child to keep his eyes on the ball, and cue him when to move his hands toward the ball. Should this prove too difficult, attach a tether ball to a string suspended from a ceiling. Swing the ball and have the child practice catching it from a stationary position. This provides a more controlled and structured experience than freely tossing the ball. The string ensures that the ball will always be at the same height in its swinging arc as it approaches the child's stationary position.

As a final step in this learning experience, use a baseball and practice catching it over increasingly wider distances. Because this is a harder type of ball, it must be thrown gently and over a short distance initially to be sure that the child's skills and fears are able to handle the experience successfully.

These two examples of task structure illustrate how to present a task in a simplified manner and with explicit cues to ensure successful performance. An SLD child may need to have many tasks presented with this type of structure in order to guarantee a higher degree of success.

Situational Structure

Do not assume that a situation will be easy for an SLD child to handle, even though it seems easy for others, including younger siblings. Carefully select, control, and monitor each situation to which the SLD child is exposed. Maximize the child's chances for successful performance in each experience.

Parents and teachers select or create many experiences for children to provide entertainment or educational enrichment. Birthday parties, family reunions, joining a swim club, visiting a museum, attending cultural events, going to the circus, shopping, eating at a restaurant, and traveling are but a few of such experiences. Unfortunately, an SLD child may not be able to handle these experiences in a way that is either entertaining or enriching.

You may feel that you are neglecting the SLD child by not providing him with the same experiences most children have in growing up. If these experiences result in upset feelings, temper tantrums, or fearfulness, however, the recreational and educational value of the experience will be lost. Some of the situations may need to be completely avoided at certain stages of the child's development or at least presented in a modified form. Methods for providing situational structure include the following:

• *Do not expose the SLD child to situations where failure is anticipated.* Remember that losing control of feelings is one type of failure. Carefully select or modify situations to ensure a successful outcome. A birthday party might involve one friend, not twelve. A circus or parade might be watched on TV, which can be turned off if necessary, not amidst large crowds with much noise and stimulation. Eating in restaurants might occur in the fast food/take-out type, not in an elegant candle-lit type.

• *Prepare the child in advance for every situation that is not part of the usual daily routine.* Preparation should occur for both pleasant and unpleasant situations. Many people feel uncomfortable in an unfamiliar situation or whenever their expected role is not clearly defined. Such discomfort is also experienced by SLD children, but with more intensity. How far in advance the preparation is offered will depend upon the child's ability to live with the anticipation of an event. Some SLD children can handle anticipation several days in advance of an event. Others can handle the anticipation only one day, a few hours, or even a few minutes. Generally, however, the events that will be more difficult for the child to handle emotionally should be given more advanced preparation time.

• *Explain clearly to the child what can be expected in a situation.* Do not attempt to deceive the child. If the child is being taken to the dentist, for example, don't pretend to start out for a pleasure ride in the car and then just happen to end up in front of the dentist's office. If the child is going to the doctor for a shot, do not say that the shot will not hurt.

Every shot hurts, at least a little bit. When you have been through many upsetting experiences with an SLD child in the past, it is very natural to want to avoid additional confrontations. You may think that by not discussing a difficult situation in advance (such as telling the child that the shot will hurt a little), it will make the situation easier to get through. Sometimes not telling the child about the discomforts to be anticipated in a situation facilitates getting through that particular situation. The child's reaction to subsequent situations, however, may become even more difficult to manage because of the anxiety over not knowing what to expect and not being able to trust what adults say.

• *Explain the expected behavior, limits, and consequences in a supportive, nonthreatening, yet decisive manner.* Let the child know what kinds of behavior are acceptable and unacceptable. Explain what the consequences will be should unacceptable behavior occur. A word of caution is needed here. The manner in which ground rules or behavioral limits are presented to the child significantly influences the success or failure of the experience. Presenting ground rules in the form of a threat sets the stage for a power struggle between the child and adult. For example, suppose a parent were to say, "Jack, you'd better not fuss when I don't buy you everything you want in the store. If you do, I'll never take you shopping again!" This message implies that Jack might be able to demand several toys or items without consequences. After all, several things is not the same as "everything." He may also remember those previous shopping trips when his mother or father bought him things so they wouldn't feel embarrassed in public by his fussing and demanding behavior. Besides, his parents could not possibly mean that they would "never" take him shopping again. They've said that before, yet he still gets to go shopping occasionally. The expected behavior and limits should be presented to the child in a manner which is supportive, nonthreatening, yet decisive. For example, before leaving home the parents might say:

Jack, we need to go shopping for a few things today. I know how difficult it is to go into the stores without touching or wanting the things that interest you. So, if you can shop with us like a big boy without fussing or crying for the things you want, we'll buy you an ice cream cone as a reward when we have finished the shopping. But if you get upset because you can't have the things you see, then we'll know that you just can't handle shopping today. If this hap-

pens, we'll come home right away, and the shopping will be done some other time when Daddy (or Mommy) can stay home with you.

Once said, it is important to follow this preestablished plan exactly, without more than one reminder should the undesired behavior begin to emerge.

• *The duration of an experience should be determined by the child's tolerance.* In all fairness to the child, the duration of any experience should be only as long as the child can reasonably be expected to maintain control. In the previous example, if it is known that the child can handle only about one hour of shopping, the parents should not plan a two hour shopping trip. The second hour will only be disastrous, the shopping will have to be discontinued (as the child was told before leaving home), and the child ends up being disciplined (no ice cream cone) because of losing control.

• *Reward appropriate behavior.* Some parents may consider the promise of an ice cream cone or other rewards for acceptable behavior to be a bribe and, therefore, undesirable. Verbal praise, however, may be too abstract for the child's maturity level to be an effective motivator. Concrete "rewards" become bribes only if parents or teachers continue to offer them indefinitely. Couple the concrete reward with verbal praise and recognition of the child's acceptable behavior. Eventually verbal praise or just the inner feeling of pride for having done well may be sufficient.

• *Avoid setting consequences that are unrealistic, vague, or will not be applied.* Such statements as "I'll never take you shopping again" or "I won't love you anymore" or "Just wait until you see what will happen to you if you don't obey me!" illustrate the kinds of consequences to avoid. The child will need to test the validity of such consequences. This will result in a power struggle. Instead, the consequences should be clearly defined, realistic, and actually applied if necessary. A reasonable consequence consistently enforced at the appropriate time helps the child learn the limits of acceptable behavior.

• *Limit the choices that the SLD child must make.* Many SLD children have difficulty making decisions or selecting from among several alternatives. Either avoid placing the child in situations that contain too many choices or reduce the number of choices or decisions the child must make. For example, selecting items from the menu in a restaurant could be confusing for the child. Instead, offer a choice between two items from among the child's preferred foods. In play situations, the child's attention span may be greater if there are only two or three toys available at any one time than if there were a toy box full of different choices. Periodically, perhaps every few days, the choice of available toys can be varied to maintain the child's interest. In school, teachers should offer two or three choices for recess activities rather than expect the child to organize free time successfully without guidelines.

• *Provide structure through the use of established procedures.* As much as possible, routine experiences at home and school (such as mealtimes, bedtimes, or reading instruction time) should follow the same procedure or set of rules each day. Repetitive exposure to an established procedure enables the child to predict what to expect and get prepared for the situation. Hopefully, the procedure will eventually become an automatic behavior pattern.

Consider mealtime behavior, for example. The established procedure might be: (a) wash hands before eating; (b) don't start to eat until everyone is seated; (c) use a fork (not fingers), and swallow one fork-load of food before trying to stuff in more; (d) do not interrupt when others are talking (but be sure to include the child in the conversation); (e) ask to have food passed rather than reaching across the table; (f) do not leave the table until excused; (g) carry your dishes to the sink.

• *Follow a relatively consistent daily schedule at home and school.* At home, the SLD child should have similar times each day for getting up, eating, playing, and going to bed. At school, teachers customarily have an established daily schedule. Teachers should be sure that the sequence of scheduled events maximizes the child's chances for success. For example, difficult tasks which require much effort or concentration should never be scheduled for afternoons when the child is fatigued or after an active recess. Such a schedule quickly elicits frustration or resistance. Effective daily schedules help the child anticipate and become prepared for events, as well as live a fairly organized life. An organized external environment enables the child to become internally organized. Internal organization facilitates behavioral control.

• *Monitor the child's behavior in each situation.* Even in carefully selected and structured situations, the SLD child often needs ongoing monitoring by an adult who can rescue the child if all does not go well. The SLD child will have good and bad days. There will be times when he will not be able to handle a situation as well as on a previous occasion. Try to recognize the warning signs and move in to provide additional support or limit the duration of the activity.

Sometimes a subtle variation of a situation makes the difference between successful and unsuccessful performance. For example, on some occasions the child might handle a particular situation quite well. On others the same situation might be poorly handled in the presence of a sibling because of jealousy, when the parent's or teacher's attitude seems irritable and impatient, or when the situation follows a failure experience or emotional upset from which the child has not fully recovered.

These examples illustrate how to provide situational structure through selecting, controlling, and monitoring the SLD child's experiences. This is an ongoing process which takes considerable time and energy. Significantly more time and energy would be necessary to manage the child's poorly controlled behavior were structure not provided.

Relationship Structure

Provide emotional support for the SLD child in an empathic, understanding manner. Demonstrate or model the kinds of behavior that will enable the child to cope successfully with his feelings and needs.

* *Through careful observation of the child, learn to recognize the early stages of an emotional upset.* Whenever these early stages are apparent, communicate to the child, either verbally or nonverbally, your understanding of the child's feelings. Do whatever seems necessary to help the child maintain control of his feelings. For example, smile warmly to express encouragement and support. Move close to the child and perhaps place your hand on his shoulder to provide reassurance. Softly comment that the task seems to be upsetting the child and offer the child just enough assistance to complete the task successfully.

* *Use honesty, fairness, consistency, and nonvindictive intervention to build a trusting relationship with the child.* A relationship based on trust provides emotional support for the child and increases the effectiveness of behavioral management techniques. Be aware of your attitude and tone of voice in all communications with the child to be sure that these are in harmony with the words that are being spoken.

* *Share with the child some of the difficult experiences or fears you have had.* Letting the child know about some of your previous failures and

fears enables him to realize that parents and teachers are not omnipotent, omniscient individuals. Even though they are not perfect, parents and teachers are able to function relatively successfully each day. The child's desire to grow up to become like the parents or a respected teacher becomes more plausible knowing that they have shortcomings, too.

• *Model appropriate behaviors for the child.* Children are usually very perceptive of adults' behavior. Because much learning takes place through imitation, be a good example for the child. The child will notice how you respond when you make a mistake, how you handle frustrating situations, and how you express various feelings. Your behavior should demonstrate that it is all right to make mistakes, that it is better to walk away from a frustrating situation than lose control, and that there are better ways to deal with anger than having a tantrum or fighting.

• *Verbalize cause-effect relationships for the child.* The SLD child may be unable to label or verbalize feelings, recognize that a particular feeling was caused by a particular event, or realize that his behavior caused the resulting outcome. These cause-effect relationships may go unnoticed unless you bring them to the child's attention. Do this tactfully and supportively to avoid adding fuel to the child's emotional fire. For example, suppose that an SLD child has had temper tantrums on several previous occasions whenever he became frustrated trying to build some object with his erector set. Building objects with this toy requires patience, fine motor coordination, the ability to follow step-by-step directions, and the ability to perceive spatial relationships. While some children enjoy this toy immensely, the SLD child may not have developed these necessary skills.

Prior to a recurrence of another tantrum, the mother might say:

Johnny, I've noticed that you get angry each time you try to build something with your erector set. It never turns out right. I know how upset it must make you feel. I've gotten angry myself whenever I've tried to make a new dress and it didn't fit well when I finished. When that happened, I got help from someone who knew more than I about sewing and making dresses. Perhaps Daddy and I shouldn't have bought the erector set for you until you were a little older when it will be easier for you. For now, play with your other toys instead. Let's put the erector set on the shelf and save it as a special toy to use whenever you want Daddy or me to play with you. That way we can help you learn how to use the set so that it won't always be hard for you.

This example illustrates both relationship structure (the manner in which the situation is explained to the child) and task structure (using the toy only with parents' help).

Hopefully the child will recognize the support, realize that his feelings are understood, and accept the structure that is presented. If so, the tantrums that always resulted for that situation will be minimized. If the child does not accept this structure willingly, the parents will have to respond accordingly. Recognize the child's disappointment, but repeat matter-of-factly the need for such structure. Supportively mention that it is temporary, not forever. Do not "give in" if another tantrum occurs in response to this structure. Permitting the child to play with the toy alone is known to be a failure situation for him. Carry through with the structure in a manner that reflects conviction, firmness, yet patient understanding. Try to divert the child's interest to an easier toy.

• *Acknowledge and praise the child's efforts and progress.* Even if a situation results in failure, the child should be praised for at least trying and for even the slightest evidence of skill development. This kind of recognition and praise helps improve the child's feelings of confidence. While recognition and praise should be given frequently, be cautious not to respond excessively or in a sugary-sweet manner. It could come across to the child as being both abasing and insincere.

PRESCRIPTIVE DOSES OF STRUCTURE

Initially, task structure, situational structure, and relationship structure may need to be used extensively. Perhaps every task, situation, and moment of the day will need to be structured to provide the child with sufficient guidelines and support to get through experiences successfully. On the other hand, some SLD children may need structure in only selective ways. Determine how much structure is needed with a particular child on the basis of day-to-day experiences. If the child's behavior is persistently difficult to manage, examine the tasks, situations, and interactions associated with this behavior. Tighter or more extensive structure may be needed, but structure is not a panacea. The use of structure will not completely eliminate all behavior management difficulties. Structure will greatly reduce the frequency and intensity of such difficulties, however.

Remain aware of daily fluctuations in the child's need for structure. Whenever the child is fatigued, ill, or under increased pressure, greater amounts of structure will be required. The type of structure will vary with the child and the situation. Provide more emotional support, reassurance, or humor at such times. Temporarily avoid difficult tasks or situations or only present them with increased assistance from adults. Present this temporarily increased structure tactfully and casually. The child may resist anything that serves as a reminder that he lacks certain skills or is unable to handle a situation that was previously handled well.

The child's need for structure will also change over longer periods of time. As skills develop that enable the child to handle a task or situation better than previously, reduce the amount of structure proportionately. Gradually increase the difficulty of tasks or situations and introduce new ones that had been previously withheld. Present new or more complex experiences in a structured manner initially. Just because the child demonstrates the ability to handle routine experiences with less structure, don't assume that he is also ready to handle new experiences with little or no structure. Present each new experience with as much structure as the child needs to handle it successfully. Reduce the structure in areas of functioning where the necessary skills are developing.

With each new task or situation, begin with more structure than is needed to ensure success. Gradually reduce the structure to the appropriate level. If a task or situation were initially presented with too little structure resulting in failure, the child may resist the adult's efforts to increase the structure. The SLD child understandably resists whatever serves as a reminder of his failures or skill limitations. Less resistance will occur if a task or situation is initially presented with more structure than necessary, provided that the structure is then reduced to the appropriate level. This demonstrates success to the child because the change is forward toward more grown-up experiences, not backward toward more simplified experiences. If you misjudge how well the child can handle a task or situation and more structure becomes necessary to reduce frustration or failure, then provide it. Any resistance from the child can usually be handled by means of relationship structure techniques (support, empathy, diplomacy, firmness, explanations, and a sense of humor).

SUMMARY SUGGESTIONS

• *Establish schedules* for daily routines so that events occur at approximately the same time each day.

- *Plan the sequence of daily routines* to avoid predictable conflicts. For example, don't schedule a chore for the child (such as feeding the dog) at the same time as the child's favorite TV program or a difficult educational task immediately before lunch, after an active recess period, or late in the day when the child is fatigued.

- *Establish specific procedures* for carrying out each routine. Develop orderly procedures for getting up, going to bed, mealtimes, recreational activities, and each classroom activity. Be explicit about the steps necessary to complete each procedure. For example, a young SLD child might have an 8:00 P.M. bedtime. His bedtime procedure might be as follows: 7:00 P.M., get undressed and take a bath; 7:30 P.M., bedtime snack; 7:40 P.M., brush teeth; 7:45 P.M., listen to bedtime story; 8:00 P.M., lights out.

- *Explain and demonstrate each procedure.* Be sure that the child understands exactly what is expected. More than one explanation and demonstration may be needed until the child can perform each procedure appropriately.

- *Adapt the complexity and duration of tasks and procedures* to the child's skill levels and attention span. Problems will develop if a task or procedure is too difficult or lasts significantly longer than the child's attention span.

- *Plan transitional activities* to fill unscheduled times. For example, the child may be ready for school several minutes before the school bus arrives or may finish an educational task before the teacher is available to assign the next task or before it is time to go to lunch. Pre-select brief activities to fill these empty times (such as assembling a small puzzle, drawing or coloring, listening to a record, looking through a picture book, or watching TV). These activities may enable the child to wait patiently for the next event in the daily schedule.

- *Eliminate distractions* as much as possible. Minimize objects or sounds that interfere with concentration and successful completion of tasks. The child's desk top should contain only the materials necessary for the task at hand. The child's desk should be positioned to reduce visual distractions or to facilitate monitoring by the teacher.

- *Be consistent but not inflexible.* Occasional deviations from established procedures may be necessary because of the child's needs or other reasons. If the deviations represent a significant change in the child's routine, be prepared to offer the necessary support to help the child adapt.

- *Be firm but not uncaring.* Make it clear through words or actions that you are in charge of situations, but also that your methods are selected out of concern and respect for the child.

- *Avoid arguments and power struggles* with the child. Don't feel defensive about enforcing a procedure or limit if it was carefully selected with the child's needs in mind. If the child resists, listen and consider his point of view, then state your decision about how the situation will be handled. Avoid long explanations, discussions, or pleading. Sometimes a power struggle can be side-stepped by casually and briefly changing the subject to a neutral topic. Then, just as casually, continue enforcing the procedure or limit that the child had been resisting.

- *Don't be afraid to admit mistakes.* If you feel that you mishandled a situation, be willing to admit this to the child. Modify your response the next time a similar situation occurs. This provides an excellent role model for the child. It demonstrates that it is not the end of the world to make mistakes, and that behavior can change as we learn from experience.

- *Avoid blaming yourself* for the child's problems or lack of progress. Feeling guilty only uses up valuable energy that can be used more productively by providing the child with educational and emotional assistance.

- *Keep a healthy sense of humor.* Try to maintain perspective so that each incident does not appear catastrophic. Laughter sometimes clears the atmosphere and reduces the tension. Include the child in the laughter, but make it clear through some verbal or nonverbal expression of warmth and acceptance of the child that you are laughing with him, not at him. The hypersensitive SLD child might otherwise interpret your laughter to mean that you are mocking or ridiculing him.

Therapeutic Discipline

"Sparing the Rod Doesn't Spoil the Child"

chapter fourteen

DEFINITION OF THERAPEUTIC DISCIPLINE

The terms *discipline* and *punishment* are frequently used synonymously with little or no differentiation. The definitions of these terms do overlap in that both may refer to chastisement for a wrongdoing. There is an important distinction between these terms, however, which should also be reflected in your attitude toward the SLD child. Punishment connotes the vindictive use of a penalty for an intentional disobedience. Discipline connotes a form of training that attempts to correct, mold, or strengthen behavioral responses.

Therapeutic discipline can be defined as the methods of training which (1) attempt to correct, mold, or strengthen a child's behavioral responses, (2) are prescriptively selected to be relevant to the child's developmental levels, and (3) are applied in a manner that reflects empathic understanding of the child's needs. Through trial and error, many parents and teachers have discovered that therapeutic discipline is often more effective than various forms of punishment when dealing with the behavioral problems of SLD children.

Factors That Influence
the Effectiveness
of Therapeutic Discipline

● *Be aware of your attitude when applying discipline.* A basically effective disciplinary method will be relatively useless if your attitude reflects sarcasm, indifference to the child's needs or feelings, or some other form of rejection. This does not mean that you should not feel annoyed if the child misbehaves. Make it clear to the child, however, that it is the misbehavior that is disliked, not the child.

● *Avoid getting into power struggles with the child.* If you feel the need to "prove" your authority over the child, you have probably already lost control of the situation. The adult's authority is implicit in every parent-child and teacher-child interaction. Were it not, the child would not feel the need to "test" the limits or durability of the authority.

Simply remain firm with the enforcement of limits rather than trying to "defend" your authority or "prove" that you are in control of a situation. If the child sees that he has placed you on the defensive, he is likely to enjoy the victory and push the battle as far as possible. If this happens, the child may also feel anxious about having such power at his young age. This could lead to a more frantic testing of limits until he finds the security of firm boundaries.

● *Be sure that the expectations established for the child are appropriate.* A child might misbehave whenever expectations are inappropriate for his skills or tolerance levels. A task that seems very difficult or prolonged might provoke a rebellious response from the child. Regardless of how the adult perceives a task, it is the child's perception of the task or of the adult's expectations that determines the child's response.

The child's limited self-confidence, patience, and frustration tolerance will cause him to perceive the situation quite differently from the adult. Keep your expectations fair and realistic so that the child will not feel overburdened.

● *The adults involved with the child should establish similar expectations and consequences for misbehavior.* Without consistency, it will take the child considerably longer to learn appropriate patterns of behavior and control. The child becomes confused if one parent or teacher tolerates a behavior that another parent or teacher disciplines. Which expectations should be followed? Which limits should be respected? Which adult represents the top authority? Can one adult be manipulated against the other? These and other questions in the child's mind interfere with his efforts to adapt.

Most "normal" children can adapt to inconsistencies in daily life. They are able to evaluate situations quickly and accurately and decide how to respond appropriately. SLD children often lack sufficient skills for making quick and accurate decisions and adaptations. If they can't decide how to react appropriately, their responses will probably be inappropriate.

CONSEQUENCES FOR BEHAVIOR

Most children are able to learn cause-effect relationships from the things that happen to them as a result of their behavior. Both positive and negative behaviors elicit some kind of consequence or response from others. If a child obeys his parents, he is praised; if he disobeys, he is disciplined. Generally, the behaviors that are rewarded, encouraged, or gratifying in some way will occur again. Similarly, behaviors that are not rewarded or gratifying or that are disciplined will gradually be extinguished. This is a simplistic statement, but essentially accurate. This type of learning must occur in order for a child to develop the inner controls necessary for socialized behavior. Many SLD children seem to have difficulty perceiving how their behavior may cause other things to happen. For example, an SLD child might exclaim, "I don't know why Joe got so mad at me when I tripped him. I was just kidding." To help the SLD child understand cause-effect relationships and develop inner controls, consider the following suggestions.

• *Select consequences that are relevant to the child's behavior.* Relevant consequences help the child understand the connection between behavior and outcome. For example, if the child deliberately breaks a window, he should be expected to pay a reasonable amount toward its replacement. The money can be deducted from the weekly allowance or earned by doing extra chores. If the child hits a classmate during recess play, for example, he should be deprived of the remainder of that recess period. The teacher should explain to the child that because he did not handle recess appropriately, he will be given some time to think of a better way to express the anger he felt toward the classmate. At the end of this "time out" period, the teacher should discuss the incident with the child to find out if he thought of a better way to express his anger. If so, the child should be praised for his good idea and encouraged to try it the next time he feels angry. If not, the teacher should suggest alternative responses to hitting someone, such as discussing his feelings with the teacher or walking away from the activity until he "cools off" and regains control of his feelings.

Apply the consequences in a manner that not only communicates the desire to help the child learn more appropriate behaviors, but also expresses regrets that facing the consequence is the only possible course of action. Avoid applying consequences in a manner that suggests it is being done primarily because of your anger or need for retaliation.

The reasons for a particular consequence should be discussed with the child. This makes the connection between the behavior and the consequence more obvious and easier to learn. Keep the discussion brief and simple enough to be understood by the child.

• *Provide positive consequences for appropriate behavior.* If you focus primarily upon the child's inappropriate behaviors, most of your interactions with him will become negative and disciplinary. Every child needs attention from adults. If the only attention available is in the form of discipline, the child may behave inappropriately simply to receive whatever attention he can. Such interactions do not improve the child's self-esteem.

Sometimes the child's appropriate behaviors are taken for granted and not acknowledged. Sometimes we expect the worst from the child, and the child meets our expectations. Instead, place your primary emphasis upon the child's appropriate behaviors. Try to increase the frequency of positive consequences (warm smile, praise, extra time with a favorite activity, increased privileges commensurate with more grown-up behaviors) and decrease the frequency of negative consequences. This does not mean that you should ignore inappropriate behaviors, but that you should become more aware of the child's appropriate behaviors and respond accordingly. Recognize the child's efforts to do well (even if his efforts fail), praise even small accomplishments, and reward desirable behaviors. When appropriate behaviors are just developing, it is particularly important to offer positive consequences to support and encourage the child during this difficult stage of learning. The more the child's self-esteem is enhanced, the more easily he can face new learning experiences with a sense of confidence rather than a fear of failure.

- *Focus the child's efforts upon a limited number of behaviors at any one time.* It would be overwhelming and unrealistic to expect the child to work on eliminating all inappropriate behaviors at the same time. Focus upon two or three of the most problematic behaviors until sufficient improvement takes place in response to structure and relevant consequences. As each inappropriate behavior improves to a satisfactory degree, shift your attention to another inappropriate behavior that needs improvement. Similarly, focus upon two or three appropriate behaviors that are just developing and provide positive consequences to help the child strengthen them.

Some inappropriate behaviors will be resistive to change until the child develops the skills that are needed for appropriate alternative behaviors. Until such skills develop, make life more tolerable by reducing the intensity and frequency of these inappropriate behaviors through the use of structure as described earlier.

- *Develop preestablished consequences.* Give forethought to the selection of consequences for both acceptable and unacceptable behaviors. Having preestablished consequences reduces the chances that appropriate behavior will pass unnoticed, and that inappropriate behavior will elicit vindictive reactions from adults. Whenever possible, the child should be included in the decision-making process to select consequences. Although you will need to guide discussion along realistic channels and tactfully make the final decision, seriously consider and show respect for the child's input.

- *Avoid impulsive selection of consequences for inappropriate behavior.* Impulsively selected consequences for inappropriate behavior are often influenced more by the parent's and teacher's upset feelings of the moment than by the child's needs for guidance. Parents and teachers need not have all the answers, nor must they make decisions immediately when faced with some type of problem. Should you feel unsure about how to respond to the child concerning an inappropriate behavior, say you need time to decide what should be done. The word *time* here refers to a few minutes until you have regained composure or thought the situation through, not several hours or "when your father gets home." This type of momentary delay helps the adult select a consequence that is less likely to make the immediate situation worse. It also provides the child with the desirable model to "think before you act."

• *Avoid negative consequences that are harsh, prolonged, vague, or unenforceable.* For example, if the child misbehaves in a restaurant, the consequence should not be that you will "never take him anywhere again," that he cannot go to a restaurant again for "one year" or until he "grows up," or that you "won't love him anymore." Consequences like these invite the child to test the limits to see if you really mean what you say and do not communicate your desire to help. Be sure that the consequences are equally enforceable by parents, teachers, or other involved adults.

• *Remind the child of the preestablished consequences prior to a recurrence of a specific behavior.* Select a time when the child seems sufficiently controlled to listen attentively. Express your awareness of the difficulty the child had controlling his behavior in a particular situation. Refer to a specific occasion that exemplifies what you mean. Specifically explain the kinds of behavior that would be more appropriate or acceptable in that situation. Then remind the child of the consequence that will be used should the inappropriate behavior occur again. Stress your desire to help the child learn to behave like a "big boy" or "big girl."

For example, a father might say to his son just prior to dinner:

Johnny, remember how angry you were last night at dinner when you thought that your sister's piece of pie was bigger than yours? You were so angry you grabbed her pie and knocked over your glass of milk. That's why I had you sit on the chair in the hall until you could calm down enough to join us again at dinner. Try to remember that tonight at dinner so that you won't have to sit on the chair again. We want you to eat with us, but not when you misbehave. If you are hungry enough to eat more than mother gives you, show us what a big boy you are by just asking for more food when you finish what you have. Are you willing to try that?

The manner in which these issues are discussed must be geared to the child's level of understanding and readiness to accept what is presented. This does not mean that if the child will not accept the consequence, it should not be discussed or applied. Rather, discuss the consequence in a manner that the child can understand without lowering his self-esteem. Such a manner presents the adult as someone who understands and wants to help the child, rather than someone who simply wants to boss and get revenge for the child's misbehavior. The latter type of presentation will immediately elicit a power struggle in many cases.

Respond similarly to appropriate behaviors that are just developing. Tell the child you have noticed how well he has been trying to handle a particular situation, that you know how proud that must make him feel, and that it isn't easy to do something well when it is first being learned. This type of praise may be all that is needed to reinforce the behavior and encourage it to happen again. Some SLD children may need a more specific or concrete type of consequence or reward to reinforce positive behaviors. Verbal praise may be too abstract to be meaningful or reinforcing for some of these children. In such cases, discuss the reward you will provide the next time this positive behavior occurs. Remind the child of the potential reward just prior to a recurrence of the situation for which that behavior is appropriate.

Don't offer these rewards as bribes. Instead, select the rewards so that they symbolize "growing up," and give the child's efforts a helpful boost. Occasionally the recognition for appropriate behavior will be more effective if given spontaneously, without having previously informed the child. The important point, however, is that appropriate behavior must be given its fair share of recognition. Don't just focus upon disciplining inappropriate behavior. Preestablished consequences for acceptable behavior help you become more cognizant of the things the child is doing right. It is so easy to overlook behavior that is not causing problems. From the child's viewpoint, recognition for positive effort is very important.

● *Be consistent in the use of consequences.* Consistent use of consequences defines the limits of acceptable behavior. Without this consistency, the child may respond more frequently with unacceptable behaviors in his efforts to define the limits. If a child occasionally gets his way by throwing a tantrum and sometimes gets removed from the situation until he regains control, tantrums may continue to occur because they occasionally get him what he wants. On the other hand, if the child is consistently removed from the situation in which the tantrum occurs, he might decrease the frequency of his tantrums.

Newly emerging, acceptable behavior may be difficult for the child to sustain. He may need consistent encouragement, praise, or some form of acknowledgement to help him with his efforts to grow up. Inconsistent use of recognition could discourage the child from trying if "nobody really cares."

• *When enforcing a consequence, verbalize the reason for the consequence to help the child learn the cause-effect relationship.* In verbalizing a positive consequence, your message should convey pleasure with the child's behavior and feelings of pride for the child. Depending upon the situation, this may or may not be followed by a specific reward, such as a special treat. Obviously a special reward cannot follow every piece of appropriate behavior, but verbal praise or recognition should be offered frequently for newly emerging patterns of acceptable behavior. For example, a mother might respond to her daughter setting the table for dinner by saying, "Mary, I really appreciate your helping me with dinner by setting the table. I feel very proud of the way you are doing things like this to help me. You are becoming a big girl, which should make you feel proud of yourself, too."

On the other hand, when verbalizing a negative consequence, express your displeasure with the child's behavior but acknowledge the possibility that the child may not have been able to control his behavior better. Verbalize to the child his ability to learn how to change this inappropriate behavior and explain that the reason for the consequence is to help him learn what is acceptable. The negative consequence should then be enforced. For example, a student disrupts the classroom by making inappropriate noises that cause the other students to laugh. After having the student step outside the classroom with her, the teacher might respond by saying:

> *Tom, it makes me angry when you disrupt the class in that way. You are delaying your progress as well as that of everyone else in class. I know some of this work is difficult for you and perhaps you thought it could be avoided by disrupting the whole class. However, the work is important and cannot be avoided. I want you to make up the time you wasted by finishing your work during recess time today. From now on, should you ever need help with difficult work, just raise your hand and I'll be glad to help.*

CRISIS INTERVENTION PROCEDURES

Many parents and teachers conscientiously try to provide SLD children with structure, emotional support, and skill development opportunities.

Their efforts, with varying effectiveness, reduce the frequency and intensity of problem behaviors. Nevertheless, these children still respond occasionally with frustration, negativism, emotional upset, and power struggles. What can be done when these behaviors occur? Again, the specifics of how to respond depend upon the child and the situation, but the following guidelines may prove helpful.

• *Learn to recognize the subtle cues that signal the beginning of a negative reaction.* The more familiar you are with the child, the easier it will be to detect subtle changes in the child's behavior that are indicative of an imminent emotional upset. Perhaps restlessness will increase, interest may wane, or irritability may develop.

• *Try to prevent the child's negative reaction from becoming more intense.* Depending upon the situation, respond in one or more of the following ways: (a) place a reassuring hand on the child's shoulder; (b) casually offer to assist the child; (c) offer a supportive comment; (d) suggest a less frustrating task or divert the child's attention to a different topic or situation; (e) suggest taking a break to do something more enjoyable; or (f) introduce a little humor to lessen the subjective importance of the situation.

• *Remind the child of the limits and expectations.* If the child's negative reaction continues to escalate, in spite of your attempts to "nip it in the bud," express your concern that he is becoming upset or behaving inappropriately. Remind the child of the behavior you expect. Offer these reminders in such a manner that others (peers or adults) do not overhear your comments, and the child does not feel compelled to continue his behavior just to save face. Give the child two choices: either pull his behavior together by exerting better controls (with or without your assistance) and remain in the situation or leave the situation until his behavior is under better control. For example, a teacher might say:

> *Peter, you are becoming too upset with this math assignment, and you are disturbing the other children. Just do the best you can and don't worry if you make mistakes. I'm right here if you need my help. If you are unable to control youself and work more quietly, then I'd like you to go to the time-out area until you get over being upset.*

● *Provide the child with a "time-out" area.* Sometimes we all need to get away from a difficult situation to regain composure or think about how we can respond better the next time we face the same situation. If the child is becoming upset, he might regain control quickly if allowed to go to some neutral place alone for awhile, such as the bedroom or an isolated area in the classroom. Perhaps a five minute "time-out" period could be a preestablished procedure for the child to use voluntarily to prevent losing control or as a consequence for an emotional blow-up.

● *Use physical intervention with a minimum amount of force.* If it appears that the child's inappropriate behavior will be prolonged, especially in the classroom situation, remove the child from the situation to minimize upsetting or disrupting the other children. Should the child resist leaving the situation and continue to display inappropriate behavior or emotional upset, he may need to be physically assisted to leave. Physical intervention is also occasionally necessary to prevent the child from being hurt, hurting others, or to prevent property damage. Use only the minimum amount of force necessary to handle the situation without physically hurting the child.

While applying physical force or restraint, verbalize to the child in a calm and matter-of-fact way that you will help control his behavior only until he regains control and no longer needs such help. As the child signals increased control (struggling stops, tension relaxes), your restraint should lessen proportionately. Be prepared to reapply physical restraint should the child's apparent self-control be a manipulation in order to resume the inappropriate behavior. Again, the kind of relationship that exists between the child and yourself prior to using physical intervention will be a significant factor in determining the child's response. In general, the more positive the relationship, the easier it will be for the child to accept your help, and the quicker he will regain control.

● *Discuss the incident with the child after control has been regained.* The discussion should be casual and serious, but not a lecture filled with criticism or threats. The content of the discussion should recognize the child's upset feelings, the apparent reason for them, and suggestions for more appropriate ways to respond the next time a similar situation occurs.

For example, suppose an SLD child is trying to fix the chain on his bicycle, and the task is too difficult for him. He becomes frustrated, enraged, and throws the bicycle onto the driveway, bending the wire basket, which makes him even more enraged. His mother hears the commotion and comes to see what happened. Rather than scolding her son for mis-treating his bicycle, which would only make matters worse, she might respond by saying:

> *I can understand why you are angry. I get angry sometimes, too, if things don't go the way I planned. But you were trying to do some-thing that is too difficult for you right now. Even I wouldn't be able to fix a bicycle chain. So, put the bike in the garage and your father will help you fix it after supper. He can probably show you how to straighten the basket, too. I know it's fun to try new things for your-self, but the next time you try something that is too hard or that makes you angry, try walking away from it for a while or ask us for some help. Does that seem to make sense to you?*

Once again, the adult's attitude must communicate empathic concern, not resentful sarcasm. Hypersensitive children are more inclined to "hear" the adult's attitude than the words, regardless of how carefully selected the words may be.

• *If a child mishandles a situation, provide other opportunities to try again.* After the child regains control and is made aware of more appro-priate ways to respond as well as the consequences for repeated mishan-dling, provide the opportunity to try again. Perhaps your supportive assistance will help the child ease back into the situation more comfort-ably or more successfully. If the second attempt is more successful, fine. Should the inappropriate behavior *recur*, then the established consequence must be enforced. The consequence, of course, will vary with the situation. The consequence may simply be removal from the mishandled situation for the rest of that day. It may involve the loss of a related privilege for a specified period of time or simplifying the situation and providing more structure for the child the next time.

• *Don't be overly concerned if you handle a situation incorrectly.* If you overreact to a child's behavior or set consequences which later seem inappropriate, don't feel "trapped" by your decisions or guilty about your response. You probably responded the best you could at the moment. Your love and concern for the child will at times be overshadowed by your own frustrations.

We all make mistakes. The caring adult tries to discover those mis-takes and improve upon them. Explain to the child that after thinking the situation over, you decided that perhaps you reacted in the wrong way. Then explain what would have been a better response. A child can usually accept this type of explanation from adults. This shows the child that adults can make mistakes, that they are trying to be fair, and that there is a chance to grow up to be like them. It is easier to be like someone who makes mistakes than someone who is perfect.

FOLLOW-UP DISCUSSIONS

Behavior management is an ongoing process, not something that takes place only at the times when discipline is needed. The lines of communication must be kept open between parent, teacher, and child with the behavior management issues constantly in the foreground. This does not mean that you should always be reminding the child of his behavior problems. That would certainly be asking for trouble. Instead, make occasional comments about the child's progress, your understanding of the child's feelings or needs, your feelings and needs, and the cause-effect relationships that require occasional reinforcement. Make these comments in a casual, low-key manner with an empathic, supportive attitude.

For example, at a time when the child seems relatively content, comment about how enjoyable he is to be with at that moment or contrast the child's present behavior with the greater behavioral problems experienced several months ago. Because progress takes place so slowly, it is difficult for the child to see the results of his efforts. By contrasting the child's improved behavior with previous behavior, you not only help the child to appreciate the progress, but also tell him that you recognize it. For example, if you have a new idea about why the child may have had a previous emotional blow-up, discuss this idea with the child to get his opinion. This shows a respect and understanding for the child which can be very supportive.

These types of discussions strengthen your relationship with the child and facilitate the management of the next behavioral problem. Such discussions also help the child obtain a better understanding of cause-effect relationships and develop inner controls over his behavior. As inner controls develop, the child will be better able to discuss feelings rather than act them out inappropriately.

Variable Rates of Development

"My Child Is Ten Years Old, Going on Six!"

chapter fifteen

REMAIN AWARE OF THE
CHILD'S SKILL LEVELS

Our skills and behavior are constantly changing. They improve with maturation and learning or regress because of disuse or emotional pressures.
Changes generally occur more rapidly in childhood when new skills are
periodically emerging than in adulthood when the rate of development has
leveled off. Most children are continually broadening the range of experiences or situations that they can handle successfully. The rate at which
this occurs is usually commensurate with increasing chronological age. As
a result, an average six-year-old child will be able to handle situations as
well as most six-year-old children. When the same child is ten years old, he
will be able to handle situations as well as most ten-year-old children.

Unfortunately, this is not true for most SLD children. Their rate of
skill development or emotional maturation is usually not commensurate
with their chronological age. Their chronological age, therefore, cannot be
used as the basis for deciding which tasks or situations they should be able
to handle successfully. Because many SLD children present the outward
appearance of being relatively normal, they are frequently expected to

possess all the normal skills for their age. In view of their many hidden skill deficits, SLD children are placed under excessive pressure by such expectations. Their response to this pressure often leads to some form of failure.

Remain aware of an SLD child's skill levels in order to minimize his failure experiences as he improves his skills and learns to handle new situations. Select tasks or situations that are appropriate for the child's current skill levels, not his chronological age. Techniques were described in Chapter 11 for recognizing or identifying the symptoms of a specific learning disability. Use these techniques on a fairly regular basis so that the complexity of tasks can be varied to be compatible with an SLD child's increasing skill levels.

If tasks or situations are too difficult, the child will not experience a reasonable degree of success. If tasks or situations are overly simplified, the child will have little or no opportunity for skill development. Some degree of effort should be expected from the child, but the amount of effort will have to be geared to that child's ability to tolerate such pressure. The child's response is a fairly reliable indicator to let you know whether or not the amount of pressure needs to be adjusted.

ANALYZE YOUR COMPLAINTS

Another step in the process of assessing the SLD child's skill levels is to analyze your own complaints about him. By definition, a complaint refers to sources of dissatisfaction, irritation, or grief. Relative to an SLD child, the complaints of parents and teachers may include the child's slow rate of progress, irritating behavior patterns, and numerous demands. A careful and candid analysis of these complaints may provide additional information to guide your attempts in understanding the child and responding in ways that will improve the situation.

● *The child's skill weaknesses.* The source of some complaints may be the child's skill weaknesses. Low frustration tolerance may cause the child to respond with frequent temper tantrums. Limited skills may lead to excessive dependency upon adults. Low self-esteem and poor emotional controls may produce much irritability and limit-testing. Whenever the child's skill weaknesses appear to be the primary reason for complaint, take appropriate steps to improve the child's manner of functioning. Such steps would include the use of structure, the selection of tasks compatible with skill levels, the use of emotional support, and the providing of opportunities for skill development.

• *Adult-child interaction problems.* Many complaints are associated primarily with adult-child interaction problems. These problems frequently involve power struggles that emerge because of a combination of the child's behavior and the adult's response to that behavior. Arguing with the child, needing to prove one's authority, expecting respect from the child without earning it, or taking the child's behavior too personally only serve to escalate the intensity of a negative interaction. A winner seldom emerges from such interactions. Instead, develop preestablished consequences for persistent unacceptable behavior and apply these consequences without getting into a lot of unnecessary discussion. Enforce a consequence in a low-key, matter-of-fact, but firm manner to avoid provoking the child even further. Responding otherwise could keep the power struggle going. To reduce the frequency of adult-child interaction problems, take an honest look at yourself and eliminate the things you do or say that contribute to power struggles. Arguing, yelling, sarcasm, pleading, oversensitivity, and a lack of consistent limits and consequences rank high on the list of reasons for power struggles.

• *The adult's personal problems.* Don't overlook your own personal problems which may be contributing to your complaints about the child. Personal problems limit your tolerance for the child's behavior. Arguments with your spouse, pressures from your job, personal dissatisfactions, or physical illness are some of the problems that can limit your effectiveness in dealing with the child. Your aspirations for the child may also be too high. This frustrates the child and leaves you feeling dissatisfied. To improve such situations, focus your efforts upon resolving these personal problems, not upon changing the child in some way.

• *Irritating "normal" behavior.* Keep in mind that parents and teachers occasionally have complaints even about children who are developing normally. The normal course of development leads children through various patterns of behavior or adult-child interactions that cause dissatisfaction, irritation, or grief. Because some of the SLD child's behavior deviates from the norm, do not assume that all of the child's problem behavior is abnormal for his age. For example, a ten-year-old boy might have reading skills at a six-year level, language skills at an eight-year level, but social skills at a ten-year level. Even though he can react age-appropriately to many social situations, his age-appropriate behavior may at times be troublesome and irritating.

Some of the "problem" behavior may fall within the range of "normal expectations" for a child's level of development. A ten-year-old SLD child whose social skills are at a six-year level may at times behave in ways relatively typical of six-year-old children, even though some of the behaviors may be troublesome for parents and teachers. Lowering your social expectations for the child to a level that is normal for six-year-olds may improve the situation.

What you do about your complaints will be determined by their source. After analyzing the source of your complaints you may be able to respond to the child in ways that will lead to more effective adult-child interactions.

PROVIDE PRESCRIPTIVE OPPORTUNITIES FOR SKILL DEVELOPMENT

Normal children develop social, perceptual, and coordination skills with seemingly little conscious effort. Many SLD children develop these skills after much deliberate effort and under specially arranged conditions. To learn how to catch a ball, for example, an SLD child may require significantly more practice sessions spread over a longer period of time than most children of the same age. In addition, this child may also need to use larger, slower moving balls during much of the learning process, along with much emotional support and minimally competitive or stressful conditions. Even with all this assistance, the child's catching skills may never reach the level of competence displayed by peers.

Similarly, to learn how to respond appropriately to various social situations, an SLD child may require considerable practice, simplified situations, brief time intervals, and much structure and support. For example, the child may be unable to handle successfully a birthday party with ten guests which lasts three hours and includes several competitive games. A more successful experience may result from a party with one or two guests which lasts one hour and involves a limited number of structured games carefully selected to match the child's skills.

Provide the SLD child with opportunities for improving skills by carefully selecting or adapting situations to the child's levels of development. Repeated exposure to complex or stressful situations contributes little to the child's skill development, but much to frustration, discouragement, power struggles, and behavior problems. Learning occurs best under conditions leading to success, not failure.

Be cautious not to overprotect the SLD child as you try to minimize failure and frustration. Prescriptively selecting situations that are compatible with the child's skill levels does not mean that the child should never be exposed to failure or frustrating experiences. The degree of failure or frustration, however, should be controlled. If the child's experiences are all within the boundaries of established skills, there is little opportunity to practice more advanced skills. As the child's skills develop, expose him gradually to increasingly complex situations. This provides the child with a sense of achievement, increased self-confidence, and a feeling of pride that he is allowed to face more "grown-up" experiences.

Parents often feel apprehensive about giving their normal children increased independence as they progress through successive steps of development. Parents sometimes retain a feeling of protectiveness even as these children enter adulthood. Because SLD children typically require more than the usual amount of help and guidance during their formative years, their parents experience even greater apprehension each time these children signal the desire for more independence. As is true for any child, the SLD child needs room in which to grow and put emerging skills into practice. It is the responsibility of parents and teachers to provide the SLD child with prescriptive opportunities to develop skills and to "let go" gradually as the child demonstrates increased competence.

If absolute failure results from allowing the child to try a new experience or assume an increased responsibility, curtail the activity and evaluate the situation. Try to determine the reason for the failure. If the failure was due to insufficient structure or too large an increase in task difficulty, make the necessary adjustments and let the child try again. If the failure was due primarily to the child's limited skills, avoid the activity temporarily and focus upon helping the child develop the required skills. Supportively explain to the child that you will help him develop the necessary skills before trying the same experience again. With support from adults, the SLD child can frequently absorb a failure experience without becoming too discouraged about trying again.

ALLOW TIME FOR CHANGES TO OCCUR

We all have characteristic ways of responding to daily experiences and stress situations. Over the years, we have learned to respond in ways that make us feel most comfortable, not in ways that will make us feel more anxious, fearful, or embarrassed. The specific behavioral responses we learn are influenced by our levels of emotional maturity. If we were simply told to change our ways of responding or to handle stress in a more mature manner, this would not be an easily accomplished task. If we had sufficient time and motivation to change, along with counseling and supportive assistance, we might accomplish the change successfully.

Similarly, the SLD child's responses to daily experiences and stress developed over a period of time and reflect the child's level of emotional maturity. Few significant behavioral improvements can be expected from simply telling the SLD child to "Stop doing that!" Instead, the child will need the motivation to change, counseling and supportive assistance from adults, and time to practice and develop a different behavioral response. Because change takes time, don't abandon a behavior management technique if immediate improvement is not apparent.

Behavior management techniques vary in their effectiveness with different children and different situations. The effectiveness of these techniques is highly dependent upon the adult-child relationship. If a particular technique does not produce the desired results, consider ways to improve the relationship and trust between you and the child before deciding too quickly to change the technique. Children may also outgrow a particular technique or need a new spark of interest to maintain their motivation to change. As your understanding of the child improves, you should be able to decide whether your behavior management techniques or your relationship with the child should change.

Recognize the Needs of Other Family Members

"Sometimes I Come First!"

chapter sixteen

THE SLD CHILD'S NEEDS
SHOULD NOT DOMINATE THE FAMILY

The behavior of each SLD child demands the attention of others in various ways. Adults may need to provide nearly constant vigilance to help the child maintain acceptable control, interact appropriately, or focus attention. Family members may devote much of their time and energy to prevent or control the child's disruptive behaviors. Because of this, the SLD child can readily become the primary focus of family life. While the SLD child requires and deserves special help, try to keep a realistic perspective of the situation.

Everyone has his or her own special needs. Satisfying these needs with a reasonable frequency is important for maintaining physical and mental health. The presence of an SLD child within the family often interferes with the frequency of need gratification for other family members. If reasonable gratification of these needs is sacrificed for the apparent benefit of the SLD child, the home environment could become seriously strained.

An occasional sacrifice of family members' needs may be necessary. A modified pattern of living for all family members may be unavoidable, but it is essential to maintain perspective and provide a reasonable balance between meeting the needs of the SLD child and those of others in the family. Consider the needs of all family members in the process of developing effective behavior management techniques for the SLD child.

THE NEEDS OF PARENTS

• *Engage in recreational activities.* The SLD child's behavior management problems frequently make parents reluctant to plan recreational activities for themselves. To entertain at home could be chaotic; to leave their child with a sitter could be disastrous. The only solution, parents may decide, is to remain at home, never entertain, and stoically accept the responsibility for their child until the problems are "out-grown." While this may be one solution, there are others that can offer parents some well-deserved relaxation without neglecting their responsibilities for the child.

• *Present a united front.* Dealing with the child's behavior management problems is more tolerable if parents are united in their efforts and provide emotional support for each other. Mothers especially need this support because they generally spend considerably more time than fathers on the action front with the child. Although fathers have their share of pressures from their daily jobs, few jobs are as emotionally draining, perplexing, and frustrating as managing an SLD child's behavior for several hours. Difficult situations are easier to face when sharing them with someone else than when handling them alone. If parents use similar methods of discipline and reinforce each other's efforts, a giant step has been taken toward effective management. Parents can also provide a respite for each other when needed. Just knowing that back-up assistance is available often gives a parent a bit more of whatever it takes to "hang in there."

• *Get away from the family at times.* Everyone needs time alone occasionally to pursue special interests, collect one's thoughts, or just to collapse. Parents may find it helpful to plan such moments into their weekly schedules. One evening a week might be mother's night off and another evening might be father's. When parents cover for each other in this way, a period of relatively uninterrupted free time becomes available on some regular basis. Just knowing this can help a parent get through more difficult moments.

• *Train a reliable sitter.* Once in a while parents will want to go out together for the evening or entertain friends at home. The child's behavior need not be a reason for avoiding this. Parents should give careful attention to the selection and training of a mature sitter who can stay with the child when they are out for the evening. In fact, parents can even use a sitter if necessary when they entertain at home.

Prior to being alone with the child for some occasion, the sitter should spend time with the child when one or both parents are present. This enables the child to become familiar with the sitter, and it enables the parents to train the sitter to structure and manage the child's behavior. Perhaps several training sessions will be needed before the sitter is left in charge of the child. Not only will such training enable the sitter to handle the situation more effectively, but also the parents will enjoy their moment of relaxation more by knowing that the sitter is capable of keeping things under control.

THE NEEDS OF SIBLINGS

• *Provide other children in the family with appropriate recognition.* Parents may feel uncomfortable about praising their other children for various accomplishments in front of the SLD child out of concern for hurting the child's feelings. This is especially true whenever a younger sibling has accomplished things with which the SLD child is still struggling. The other children in the family need to experience their parents' genuine enthusiasm and spontaneity as accomplishments occur. Appropriate recognition must be given to the other children to help them develop feelings of pride and minimize their resentment of the SLD child's demands for attention.

• *Siblings have the right to privacy.* The siblings of SLD children want occasional privacy, protection of personal belongings, time to pursue special interests, and opportunities to invite their friends home. The behavior management system must take this into account. Exactly how this can be accomplished will vary from one family situation to another. It may involve family discussions, which include the SLD child, to lay down basic ground rules. It may involve careful scheduling of activities to ensure that someone is available to provide the necessary structure and supervision. It may involve establishing different, more effective disciplinary consequences that help the SLD child inhibit disruptive behavior to a greater extent. It may even involve a lock on the sibling's bedroom door to ensure better security of personal belongings.

- *Encourage positive interactions between the SLD child and siblings.* Whenever appropriate, encourage siblings to include the SLD child in their play activities. These interactions with siblings must be structured and compatible with the SLD child's skills. Also, behavioral limits must be clearly preestablished. The child must be withdrawn from the activity if these limits are broken. This kind of structure not only prevents excessive failure for the SLD child, but also provides siblings with assurance that their play activities will not be unreasonably disrupted.

REMAIN ACTIVE WITH REMEDIAL EFFORTS

Parents rarely set out to deliberately prevent or impair their child's progress, yet they often blame themselves for some of the problems. This unfounded guilt, along with feelings of despair that things will never improve, often lead parents to the point of submission. They become dedicated to the child's care at the expense of everything else. They accept whatever happens as their cross to bear. This kind of attitude typically leads to a worsening of the situation and may even contribute to the child's failures. Instead, parents must remain active in trying to provide the best types of remedial experiences for their child. They must caution themselves against wasting time and energy on feelings of guilt or despair.

If a particular technique is not effective after a reasonable period of time. (assuming that other factors, such as attitudes, are appropriate), a better one must be devised. A technique that has been effective may need periodic revisions as the child's needs change. Remediation requires ongoing effort. By remaining actively involved with this effort, parents are in a better position to stay on top of the situation, minimize the problems, and avoid feeling completely overwhelmed.

Applying Behavior Management Principles

A Model Program

chapter seventeen

The previous discussion provided a description of the characteristics or symptoms by which an SLD child can be identified as well as basic principles of behavior management. The application of these behavior management principles should enable parents and teachers to develop a therapeutic milieu within which the SLD child can realize his potential to a greater extent than would be possible in a less structured, supportive, success-oriented environment. The actual application of these basic principles can take many forms which are determined primarily by each child's specific needs, the needs of others in the environment, and the nature of the available resources.

It is impossible to illustrate every conceivable application of these principles. However, a description of the highlights of a model behavior management program may sufficiently illustrate specific techniques so that parents and teachers can more readily recognize how to adapt them to their own particular situations. This model program exists at The Pathway School in Audubon, Pennsylvania where special education and clinical services for children and adolescents with specific learning disabilities and associated social/emotional problems are provided on both a day and residential basis.

Pathway's program is designed to communicate positive regard for each child within an atmosphere that fosters the development of self-reliance so that each child becomes less and less dependent on others or on systems of behavior management for the regulation of behavior. Even though the same principles of behavior management are applied to each child, the program is individualized to meet each child's specific needs. The format of the program also varies for different age groups. The younger or developmentally less mature children are provided with extensive structure and frequent tangible reinforcements (tokens, stars, checkmarks), while the older or more intact children assume increased responsibilities for monitoring their own behaviors and are given less frequent social reinforcements (verbal praise, a smile, a pat on the back). The following example describes aspects of the program designed for the younger or developmentally less mature children.

REINFORCEMENT OF APPROPRIATE BEHAVIOR

Rationale

Positive reinforcement of appropriate behavior is an effective method not only to encourage and maintain appropriate behavior, but also to reduce the frequency of inappropriate behavior exhibited by the child. A check system is used to insure that staff members regularly provide each child with positive reinforcement and to clearly demonstrate that he is doing a good job when behaving appropriately. The system is designed to insure that the children find it very gratifying to behave appropriately whether or not social reinforcers (verbal praise, a smile, a pat on the back) are important to them. The system also fosters an appreciation for social reinforcers by pairing them with more tangible rewards when necessary.

Procedure

A behavior chart is developed for each child with input from the child. The chart lists goal behaviors the child needs to develop to improve deficit areas as well as to insure the smooth operation of the program. Perhaps four to six goal behaviors are listed for each child, some of which may be common for all the children in a particular group. Examples of goal behaviors include:

- Following rules and directions.
- Interacting positively with others.
- Taking care of responsibilities.
- Talking quietly.
- Listening carefully/paying attention.

There are boxes next to each goal behavior on the chart where checkmarks are placed. The number of boxes will vary according to the frequency of reinforcement needed by the child to develop or maintain appropriate behavior in each category. Some children need checkmarks every fifteen minutes, some every hour, some three times daily (morning, afternoon, evening).

If the child displays appropriate behavior relative to a particular category during a specified time interval, a checkmark is given in the box for that interval. If the child's behavior was not appropriate relative to a particular category during a specified time interval, no checkmark is given. Each category is reviewed in this manner for each time interval.

At a predetermined frequency (usually at the end of each day) the child may "trade-in" his chart for a specific reward if he has earned a pre-established percentage of the total possible number of checkmarks on the chart (for example, 90 percent). More frequent "trade-ins" (morning, afternoon, evening) might be needed by some children to maintain appropriate behaviors if they are unable to understand how their behavior in the morning, for example, relates to their receiving or not receiving a reward at the end of the day.

The percentage of total checkmarks which must be earned to be able to trade-in the chart for a reward should not be excessively high so as to prevent a reasonable frequency of such rewards. Perhaps initially the chart can be traded in for a reward when 75 percent of the boxes receive checkmarks. When the child is able to attain this goal consistently for a few days, the percentage of checkmarks required for a reward should be raised to 80, 85, and 90 percent in sequential steps as success is achieved at each level.

The child and a staff member jointly develop a list of acceptable, reasonable rewards that can be selected if the established percentage of checkmarks is earned. The available rewards may need to be changed periodically to maintain the child's interest. Possible rewards include:

- Spending 15 minutes alone with a staff member in a special game or activity.
- Listening to a favorite TV program.
- A slightly later bedtime.

As social reinforcers become more effective and can be used more often as a means for encouraging appropriate behavior without the accompanying checkmarks, the system can be modified to provide less frequent "trade-ins." However, "trade-ins" should probably occur no less frequently than once per week until the goal behaviors are firmly established. When the child demonstrates that he can maintain appropriate goal behaviors without relying on checkmarks, and when no other goal behaviors need to be added to the behavior chart, the child can be taken off the check system altogether. The child's appropriate behaviors should continue to be immediately reinforced by social reinforcers.

Guidelines for Using the Check System

Giving a checkmark is always accompanied by a social reinforcer, such as verbal praise and a smile, pat, or hug. However, a social reinforcer need not always be accompanied by a checkmark, especially if the social reinforcer itself is important to the child.

Many appropriate behaviors exhibited by the child can be reinforced by checkmarks. For example, behaviors characteristic of "following rules and directions" might include:

- Maintains appropriate behavior without constant reminders.
- Responds promptly to directions given by parents or teachers.
- Remains in designated areas until excused.
- Uses the property of others only with permission.
- Observes the rules of group games.
- Sits quietly during TV time or when being instructed in the classroom.

Examples of behaviors characteristic of "interacting positively with others" might include:

- Participates in group games.
- Initiates conversation.

- Responds appropriately in conversations.
- Cooperates with others.
- Interacts without verbal or physical confrontation with others.
- Displays concern for others.

Examples of behaviors characteristic of "taking care of responsibilities" might include:

- Bathes and shampoos hair efficiently.
- Dresses self independently.
- Maintains a neat appearance.
- Maintains a clean, neat room.
- Does assigned chores independently.
- Uses personal and others' property appropriately.

The child's behavior chart should be posted in a place readily accessible and visible to the child so that he can be aware of his progress.

Checkmarks should be recorded as soon as possible after being earned to emphasize the relationship between the child's appropriate behavior and the positive reinforcer.

In a school situation when other children are on the same check system, verbal praise given to those who are behaving appropriately may encourage appropriate behavior from those who are misbehaving. For example, saying, "I like the way you are behaving, John and Mary" may elicit appropriate behavior from those who are misbehaving so that they can earn similar praise (and perhaps a checkmark).

DEALING WITH INAPPROPRIATE BEHAVIOR

Rationale

Probably all children exhibit inappropriate behaviors occasionally. The child who is behaving inappropriately must be given feedback in order to become cognizant of this misbehavior and of appropriate alternative behavior. It is important that the consequence the child receives upon exhibiting an inappropriate behavior be directly and simply related to that behavior. The consequence should be administered as immediately as possible and should offer and encourage an appropriate behavior substitute. The feedback for the behavior should not include elements of humiliation or excessive criticism of the child; the consequence should not be arbitrary or physically painful. Humiliation, excessive criticism, arbitrariness, and pain serve to destroy the child-adult relationship more than to modify the behavior. Refer to Chapter 14 for additional suggestions.

Examples of Inappropriate Behavior

- Self-help skills: soiling or wetting pants; careless or inadequate bathing; sloppy grooming and dressing.
- Inappropriate vocalizations: arguing or teasing others; screaming; swearing; interrupting; lying; talking when instructed to be quiet.
- Inappropriate social interactions with others: hitting; biting; scratching; kicking; throwing objects at others; distracting others by clowning or making faces.
- Off location: getting out of seat; wandering or running around the room; leaving the room without permission; going to undesignated or "off limits" areas.
- Misuse of objects: throwing or banging objects; slamming doors; ripping objects; defacing objects; climbing on furniture; using others' property without permission; stealing.
- Inappropriate table manners: chewing with mouth open; talking with food in mouth; using fingers to eat food; playing with food or drink; throwing food.

Logical Consequences

The disciplinary action taken by the adult in response to the child's inappropriate behavior should be logically or meaningfully related to the behavior. The consequence should reflect social reality, not the adult's personal revenge or whim. The logical consequence for an inappropriate behavior may be mildly unpleasant in order to discourage the child from repeating the behavior. A logical consequence should follow an inappropriate behavior whenever possible. For example:

- If the child breaks an object belonging to someone else, he should be required to repair or replace the object with money from allowance.
- If the child spills food, he should be required to clean it up before continuing to eat.

- If the child soils his pants, he should be required to wash the soiled clothing and take a bath.
- If the child defaces a wall, he should be required to wash the wall.

Guidelines for the use of logical consequences:

- The child must see clearly that the consequence is the result of his own behavior rather than that of others. Otherwise, the act will be viewed as a punishment (which has no real connection with the behavior) rather than as a logical consequence (which does).
- The consequence should not be a retaliation ("This will teach you a lesson!") but an inevitable outcome of the behavior.
- The adult must remain a supportive, caring bystander. The adult should express genuine regret that under the circumstances the child must simply face the consequence of what he has done.
- Never use a harsh tone of voice; it connotes demands and rejection of the child.
- The adult should enforce the consequence as promptly as possible with minimal discussion. Excessive talking and explanation may reinforce attention-seeking behavior in the child. Keep the discussion simple and direct.

Time-Away Procedure

"Time-away" is the withdrawal of the child from an activity that he is handling inappropriately and temporary placement in a quiet area away from the activity. Frequently when a child is mishandling a situation or demonstrating inappropriate behaviors (screaming, hitting, negativism), a time-away period can be considered a logical consequence. That is, if the child cannot handle a situation appropriately, he is withdrawn until he is ready to respond appropriately. A time-away procedure can be used to reduce the frequency and/or severity of inappropriate behavior as well as minimize the disruption of activities at home or school.

Procedure
A. If the child exhibits an inappropriate behavior not disruptive enough to justify removal from an activity, redirect the child's attention to the task or activity. It may be helpful to reinforce other children who may be present (such as in school) for behaving appropriately in the situation by using checkmarks and/or praise.

B. If the child exhibits inappropriate behavior that is moderately disruptive, he should first be redirected to the task or activity. Again, reinforcing the appropriate behavior of other children in the situation may be helpful. If the inappropriate behavior persists, the child should be asked to leave the activity and return when he feels ready to behave appropriately.

1. If the child returns from the quiet area settled and ready to rejoin the group, he should be allowed to do so.
2. If the child settles in the quiet area but does not return after five minutes, he should be asked to rejoin the group.
3. If the child remains in the quiet area but continues to exhibit inappropriate behavior there, he should be reminded that he will be allowed to rejoin the group only after remaining quiet for five minutes.
4. If the child returns exhibiting inappropriate behavior, he should be asked to go back to the quiet area and told that he will be allowed to rejoin the group only after remaining quiet for five minutes.
5. If the child returns settled after a time-away period, but exhibits inappropriate behavior subsequently within the same activity, he should be asked to take another five minute time-away period.

C. If the child exhibits inappropriate behavior that is severely disrupttive, he should be asked to leave the activity, go to the designated quiet area, and remain there quietly for five minutes, after which he will be allowed to rejoin the activity. The seriousness of a misbehavior may warrant a more extended time-away period, such as thirty minutes to one hour.

Guidelines for the Use
of the Time-Away Procedure

A. An activity is defined as any of the following examples: mealtimes; group games; solitary play; rest periods; TV time; school tasks; group instruction.
B. The quiet area should be a neutral stimulus area, neither a pleasant nor an unpleasant place, where the child can think about more appropriate ways to respond to the mishandled activity. Avoid areas where the child can entertain himself, thus finding it a rewarding place to be.

C. In a matter-of-fact manner, the adult should remind the child of the appropriate behavior for the situation and ask him to think about that while in the quiet area.

D. If the child refuses to go to the quiet area when asked or refuses to remain there when told to do so, he should be placed in the quiet area by the adult in charge of the situation. This should be accomplished as quickly and with as little verbal or physical confrontation as possible.

E. The child's return to the group or activity should be handled as matter-of-factly as the removal. In a private, confidential manner without embarrassing the child in front of others who may be present, ask the child to explain how he plans to respond when he rejoins the activity.

Other Procedures

In certain situations it may be difficult to handle inappropriate behaviors either by logical consequences or time-away periods. A specific, realistic solution will need to be developed by the adult in charge. Examples of such situations include the following:

When several children in a classroom are exhibiting inappropriate behaviors, the on-going activity should be terminated temporarily to allow the group to settle. It is sometimes effective to turn off the classroom lights and have the children lay their heads on their desks until everyone is quiet for a few minutes. Before the activity is resumed, the children should be reminded of the appropriate behavior for the situation. Provide positive reinforcement for subsequent appropriate behavior. If the inappropriate behavior continues and the activity involves play or recess, the activity should be discontinued for that day. If the inappropriate behavior continues and the activity involves academic instruction, a logical consequence might be to make up the wasted time by using that day's recess time for instruction.

If inappropriate behavior occurs during a family outing or a classroom field trip, the child or children should be reminded of the appropriate behavior for the situation and warned that if it continues the activity will be terminated. For example, "If we can all walk quietly through the museum, we may enjoy the remainder of the exhibits. If we cannot obey the rules, we must leave." This places the responsibility on the child.

or children rather than on the adult in charge. If the situation involves only a small number of children in the classroom group, they should be taken to some waiting area and supervised while the remainder of the class finish the activity, if possible.

HOME AND CLASSROOM RULES AND EXPECTATIONS

In general, an SLD child can exhibit appropriate social behavior more successfully when guided by specific rules or procedures which make social expectations very explicit. The structure provided by rules and expectations enables the child to "read" the situation more accurately and to plan an appropriate response that will elicit positive reinforcement from others. Should the child behave inappropriately in a particular situation after becoming familiar with the rules and expectations (assuming that the expectations are realistic relative to the child's skill deficits), then the child will probably perceive the associated discipline as a logical consequence for his misbehavior rather than as the adult's arbitrary revenge. The adult in charge of a particular situation should clearly state the rules or expectations as the child is provided with opportunities to practice the appropriate behaviors. Examples of rules and expectations used at The Pathway School include the following:

1. *Bedrooms.* Children are expected to:
    a. Remain quietly in their beds before "wake-up" time until excused by the adult to wash-up for breakfast. If a child is an early riser, quiet activities such as coloring books are provided before the child goes to sleep at night with explicit instructions to play quietly in bed in the morning until it is time for everyone to get up.
    b. Remain quietly in their beds after "lights out," with the doors closed. Some children may need a night light or the bedroom door ajar for security reasons.
2. *Mealtimes.* Children are expected to:
    a. Enter the kitchen and stand quietly behind assigned seats until cued by the staff member to be seated.
    b. Remain quiet during the prayer.

    c. Wait until the staff member begins to pass the serving bowls and platters, then serve themselves and pass the food promptly but carefully.

    d. Take reasonable amounts of food that can be finished.

    e. Finish the servings taken before asking for seconds.

    f. Exhibit appropriate table manners, which means:
  1) Chew with mouth closed.
  2) Use silverware appropriately; avoid eating with fingers except when appropriate.
  3) Eat slowly and neatly.
  4) Use napkin appropriately.
  5) Converse only after swallowing food.

    g. Talk quietly, one at a time.

    h. Sit quietly until excused by the staff member to clean their places.

    i. Scrape their dishes and stack them neatly beside the sink.

    j. Exit quietly from the kitchen.

3. *Group discussions.* Children are expected to:

    a. Remain in assigned seats unless otherwise instructed.

    b. Raise their hands and wait to be called upon before entering into the discussion.

    c. Contribute appropriate comments to the discussion.

    d. Sit quietly and pay attention when others are speaking.

CHORES AND RESPONSIBILITIES

Some examples of the types of responsibilities that are assigned to children and the specific procedures to be followed when carrying them out include:

1. *Room and possessions*

    a. Bed must be made every morning; bed linens are stripped weekly and replaced with clean linens.

    b. Clothing must be kept neatly in drawers or on hangers.

    c. Toys, games, books and other possessions must be kept neatly in drawers or on shelves.

    d. Dirty clothes must be put in laundry bag; cleaned clothes must be put away in drawers or in closet.

2. *Kitchen.* On a rotating basis, two children per day are responsible for kitchen chores.
   a. Set the table.
   b. Help serve food and pour milk.
   c. Put the dirty dishes in the dishwasher.
   d. Empty the dishwasher when the dishes are clean.
   e. Sweep the floor.
   f. Empty the trash.
3. *Personal hygiene.* A formal hygiene program is maintained. Staff members provide the children with on-going individualized instruction, or assistance when necessary, in all areas of hygiene and self-help skills. For example,
   a. Daily baths and semiweekly shampoos are required.
   b. Hands must be washed before every meal; nails must be cleaned daily.
   c. Teeth must be brushed after every meal.
   d. Hair must be combed or brushed neatly before school and before meals.
   e. Clothes must be changed daily.

Children are required to complete their assigned chores and responsibilities in an acceptable manner before participating in subsequent activities. Assistance, guided practice, and supervision should be provided to the extent necessary to insure successful completion of chores and responsibilities. Positive reinforcement (checkmarks and/or social reinforcers) is provided for appropriate responses from each child. Inappropriate responses are handled by means of logical consequences and/or time-away periods.

Specific rules and procedures similar to those illustrated should be established for every situation that is a part of the child's daily routine at home and school. To the extent possible, daily schedules should also be established with specific times for each part of the daily routine. This may initially seem like a lot of unnecessary work, but the effort usually pays off in terms of a more effective behavior management system.

REKINDLE
THE FLAME

"Nothing
Lasts Forever!"

part three

Parents generally need more than suggestions of techniques or methods for helping the SLD child because they are often at the point of being unable or unwilling to try anything else. They may feel completely depleted of energy and discouraged by all previous efforts. Helping an SLD child overcome skill weaknesses and develop behavioral controls should not be the sole responsibility of one or two individuals. So many types of talent are required that parents cannot realistically provide all the necessary assistance alone.

As other resources of assistance and support are brought into the picture, the parents of an SLD child may begin to feel some relief and see signs of progress in the child. These sparks of hope enable them to rekindle the determination and dedication necessary to remain effective members of the team of professionals who are trying to help the child. Various sources of assistance and support are discussed in this section.

Sources of Help
"I Don't Know Where to Turn Next!"

chapter eighteen

If as parents you try all the suggestions discussed earlier and learn to use the behavior management techniques effectively, is that all that needs to be done? Will that be sufficient for dealing with the SLD child's behavioral difficulties and the underlying causes? Probably not. The problems usually require guidance and assistance from various specialists in addition to whatever the best intentioned parents can offer. Input from specialists should be carefully coordinated with your efforts.

Parents' dedicated, consistent, and perceptive efforts can chip away large chunks from the boulder-size problems of the SLD child, but specialized techniques are generally needed to blast away at the hard-core issues. Without help from specialists, many of the hard-core issues will remain unchanged, perhaps worsen, or become impervious to change as time passes. On the other hand, without help from parents many of the hard-core issues may be inaccessible to the efforts of specialists. Behavioral problems can become roadblocks to change. Even though some specialists are trained to resolve or modify behavioral problems, back-up assistance and cooperation from parents are essential ingredients for success.

Being an effective parent often involves using skills or techniques similar to those used by well-trained specialists, such as teachers or counselors. Even though there are similarities, there are also crucial differences. Parents cannot realistically expect to fill all roles. Even when parents are specialists themselves, such as a special education teacher or psychologist, they can seldom play the specialist's role effectively with their own child. Strong emotional ties interfere. Parents, including those specially trained in a profession, need advice and guidance from other specialists. In turn, other specialists also need advice and guidance from parents. Specialists need to know which methods parents have tried, which have been effective, and which have not. Collaborative efforts between parents and specialists combine the talents of both worlds into an optimally beneficial experience for the SLD child.

What kinds of specialists should become involved in the efforts to help an SLD child? How might one locate such specialists? What kinds of programs exist that can provide the necessary help? These questions are considered next.

PRELIMINARY EVALUATIONS

The Family Physician

As a first step, the child should be examined by the family physician to be sure that no physical problem is contributing to the various symptoms that have been noticed. If the results of a physical examination are negative, the sophisticated physician will probably refer the child to other sources for further evaluations. However, seek a second opinion if the physician responds with a statement such as, "Don't worry, he'll outgrow it!" Be very cautious about following this type of advice. Precious time can be lost by waiting for the problems to disappear. Instead of disappearing, the problems often become worse.

The Pediatric Neurologist

One of the evaluations a sophisticated physician may suggest is a neurological examination, including an electroencephalogram (EEG or brain wave test). This evaluation should be obtained from a pediatric neurologist who will determine whether or not neurological factors appear to be contributing to the child's difficulties. Frequently the results of this type of evaluation are negative. Nevertheless, it provides important baseline information that may be needed at specified intervals during the child's development. The results, positive or negative, can be useful in guiding those who will be developing a program to help the child.

Psychoeducational Specialists

A psychoeducational assessment is an essential part of the diagnostic work-up. This can be obtained at no charge through the public school system or for a fee through private facilities, such as diagnostic clinics, private schools for learning disabilities, or selected professionals in private practice. Psychologists who specialize in working with children can be a helpful resource for coordinating the psychoeducational assessment. The assessment should evaluate the child's developmental history, cognitive skills, social and emotional skills, educational achievement and learning skills, speech and language skills, and visual and auditory skills. This comprehensive assessment helps identify specific areas of strength and weakness so that a prescriptive program can be established.

Again, part or all of the psychoeducational assessment may need to be repeated at specified intervals during the child's school years. These reevaluations, supplemented with the informal assessments by the specialists working with the child, identify areas of need and rates of progress, suggest modifications in the treatment or educational program to facilitate progress, and provide data to guide the child and parents in making long-range goals.

THE PUBLIC SCHOOL SYSTEM

With the enactment of Public Law 94-142 (Education for All Handicapped Children Act) in November 1975, public schools are required by the federal government to provide a free, appropriate education for all handicapped children. This, of course, includes children with specific learning disabilities. Based upon a thorough assessment of each handicapped child's needs, the public school system (local educational agency or **LEA**) must prepare a written individualized educational program (**IEP**). The IEP explains the necessary services, annual goals, and objectives for meeting the child's special needs. Parents must approve of their child's IEP before the public school can initiate the child's program. Parents' approval must also be obtained for each annual revision of the IEP and whenever significant changes in the IEP are contemplated by the public school system. If parents do not agree with the program that the public school intends to offer their child, they have the right to a due process hearing. Parents may bring a child advocate and expert witnesses to the hearing to testify on behalf of their child's needs. Clearly, Public Law 94-142 has had a profound effect upon special education for handicapped children. The details of these regulations are presented in the *Federal Register* (August 23, 1977).

Although the public school system must provide special education programs for all SLD children, the quality of these programs is not standardized and may differ significantly from one public school system to another. Parents should obtain expert consultation if they do not know how to evaluate the merits of their public school system or what questions to ask to ensure that their child's needs are being appropriately met. Information about how to locate sophisticated consultation resources may be obtained from local chapters of the Association for Children with Learning Disabilities.

What parents interpret to be "appropriate" for their child's needs may not agree with the interpretation made by the public school personnel. Whenever there is agreement, the child can be placed in the special program designed to meet his or her needs without too much wasted time. Whenever there is disagreement, the process could become prolonged significantly with due process hearings until a resolution is reached.

APPROVED PRIVATE SCHOOLS

There are numerous private schools that offer special education programs for SLD children on a day or residential basis. Many of these schools offer programs designed for SLD children with more multiple or severe needs that can be appropriately handled by the public school system. These schools can be found in the following directories:

- *Directory of Educational Facilities for the Learning Disabled,* 8th ed. (Novato, CA: Academic Therapy Publications, 1979–80).
- *The Directory for Exceptional Children,* 9th ed. (Boston: Porter Sargent Publishers, 1981–82).
- *The Guide to Summer Camps and Summer Schools,* 21st ed. (Boston: Porter Sargent Publishers, 1979–80).

If public school officials agree that a particular SLD child needs a more intensive program than can be provided within the public school system, state educational funds might be made available to help finance the child's expenses at an approved private school. Sometimes the cost of a private school program is greater than the amount allocated by a State Department of Education. If so, funding assistance from secondary sources should be investigated, such as social welfare agencies serving children and youth, major medical insurance programs, or Supplemental Security Income (SSI) through your local Social Security office.

Whenever a private school placement is necessary, the appropriateness of such schools within the child's home state are generally considered first. If none of the available schools offer appropriate programs for a particular child's needs, then out-of-state schools are considered. A guiding principle throughout the process of finding an appropriate program for a child is to place the child in the **least restrictive environment**. This means that the handicapped child should be educated in as normalized an environment as is possible and appropriate. The nature of the least restrictive environment for one SLD child will not necessarily be the same as for another. For example, one SLD child may be able to have his special needs appropriately met by having a regular education program supplemented with assistance from a resource room teacher, while another may require an intensive special education program within a private residential school with input from multiple specialists.

SPECIALIZED SERVICES

Depending upon the range and intensity of an SLD child's special needs, a variety of specialized services may be necessary. Depending upon the necessary services available within the child's school placement (public or private), community resources may be needed to supplement the child's existing program. Each specialized service in the child's program must be prescriptively adapted to the child's needs. These services must be carefully monitored and modified as indicated by the child's progress and changing needs. Among the specialized services that might be needed by an SLD child are special education techniques, resource room or tutoring assistance, adapted physical education, speech and language therapy, perceptual-motor training, a behavior management system, individual and group psychotherapy, medication to assist emotional or behavioral control, and counseling for the child's family.

If any of the specialized services mentioned above are not available within the SLD child's school program, they might be obtained on a private basis from qualified specialists in the community. These specialists can be located through recommendations from public school personnel, special private schools or diagnostic centers, mental health clinics, or other parents of children with learning disabilities. Local chapters of the Association for Children with Learning Disabilities can be a valuable resource for meeting other parents of SLD children and obtaining useful information about SLD children.

PSYCHOTHERAPY AND COUNSELING

A few additional comments should be made concerning psychotherapy and counseling. Whenever psychotherapy and parent/family counseling are indicated, but not available within the child's school placement, these services may be obtained from a psychologist, psychiatrist, or social worker in private practice or at a mental health clinic. The type of mental health specialist selected to provide these services is less important than the type of therapeutic approach used. Typically, SLD children do not respond favorably to treatment methods utilizing introspective, nondirective, or permissive techniques designed to make the child aware of forgotten memories or experiences, especially during the early stages of treatment. The SLD child does not usually have the emotional resources or introspective ability to delve into connections between present behavior and conflicts that occurred at earlier stages of development. Instead, emotionally supportive and problem-oriented techniques within a structured setting are generally more effective.

Psychotherapy for the SLD child should provide: (1) clarification of problem areas in the home and school environments; (2) clarification and understanding of the child's feelings and needs; (3) specific suggestions for coping with stressful situations; (4) clearly defined and consistently reinforced limits; (5) appropriate reassurance and encouragement to attempt new learning experiences and develop feelings of pride and confidence; and (6) structured, short-range experiences that provide relatively immediate success so the child can build a tolerance for working toward longer range goals. These needs can often be met effectively through a combination of supportive discussions, **role playing**, and behavior modification techniques. The objectivity of behavior modification techniques minimizes the risk of power struggles and facilitates the child's understanding of cause-effect relationships.

Throughout the process of the child's therapy, parents often benefit from ancillary counseling. Such counseling should be designed to help parents obtain a better understanding of their child's needs and behavior and develop more effective methods for responding to the child. Care must be taken to avoid any implication that the parents may have caused the child's problems. Most parents respond to their child's behavior the best they can. Parents need clarification of their child's needs and specific suggestions for responding to them. If there are other issues, such as marital conflicts, which are secondary to the child's problems but contributing to them, they may need to be discussed in the parent counseling sessions also.

Depending upon the family system, other family members such as siblings may need to be included in some of the counseling sessions. The relationships between the SLD child and siblings, as well as the siblings' feelings about how their lives have been affected by the special considerations given to the SLD child, may need to be discussed. These are very real issues and must not be ignored. Just how they are dealt with will depend upon the ages and emotional integrity of family members.

SPECIALIZED ASSOCIATIONS AND RESOURCES

Association for Children with Learning Disabilities (ACLD)

The ACLD is an international organization of parents of children with various kinds of learning problems, professionals, and interested resource people. Many communities have local chapters that meet on a regular basis to discuss issues, promote projects, and support legislation related to the needs of children with learning problems. The ACLD does not endorse or recommend specific programs or specialists. Its membership, however, can offer a rich source of information to assist parents who feel completely misguided from previous attempts at finding help for their learning disabled child. If you cannot find a listing of a local ACLD chapter in the telephone directory, contact the National Association for Children with Learning Disabilities, 4156 Library Road, Pittsburgh, Pennsylvania 15234 for information about the ACLD chapter nearest to your community. An informative newsletter is published by this organization.

Other Associations and Services

The associations and services listed below are additional sources of useful information and advice concerning children with specific learning disabilities and related problems.

1. American Speech and Hearing Association
   10801 Rockville Pike
   Rockville, MD 20852
2. Closer Look: National Information Center for the Handicapped
   Box 1492
   Washington, DC 20013
3. Council for Exceptional Children
   1920 Association Drive
   Reston, VA 22091
4. Dyslexia Memorial Institute
   936 S. Michican Avenue
   Chicago, IL 60616
5. Epilepsy Foundation of America
   Suite 406
   1828 L Street, N.W.
   Washington, DC 20036
6. Learning Disabilities Program
   Bureau of Education for the Handicapped
   U.S. Office of Education
   Washington, DC 20202
7. Muscular Dystrophy Association of America
   810 7th Avenue
   New York, NY 10019
8. National Center for Law and the Handicapped, Inc.
   1236 North Eddy Street
   South Bend, IN 46617
9. National Easter Seal Society for Crippled Children and Adults
   2023 West Ogden Avenue
   Chicago, IL 60612
10. National Information Center for Special Education Materials
    (NICSEM)
    University of Southern California
    Research Annex
    University Park
    Los Angeles, CA 90007
11. New England Materials for Instruction Center (NEMIC)
    Boston University School of Education
    704 Commonwealth Avenue
    Boston, MA 02215

12. Parent Information Centers
    a. Coordinating Council for Handicapped Children
       407 Dearborn, Room 608
       Chicago, IL 60605
    b. Federation for Children with Special Needs, Inc.
       120 Boylston Street, Suite 338
       Boston, MA 02116
    c. New Hampshire Coalition for Handicapped Citizens, Inc.
       Box 1255
       Concord, NH 03301
    d. Southwestern Ohio Coalition for Handicapped Children
       3024 Burnet Avenue
       Cincinnati, OH 45219
    e. Task Force on Education for the Handicapped
       812 East Jefferson Blvd.
       South Bend, IN 46617

Bibliography

The annotated bibliography at the end of this book lists books, directories, journals, and newsletters which are useful references and sources of valuable supplemental information.

Conclusions
"From Impossible to Tolerable to Lovable"

chapter nineteen

Each child develops behavior patterns and personality traits that reflect his success in coping with the world. If the child misperceives or misunderstands experiences, is slower to develop certain skills than expected, or has erratic and immature control and adaptive ability, his behavior patterns and personality traits will reflect these limitations.

The symptoms of skill weaknesses and behavioral control problems may not be evident in the very young SLD child. As the child's development continues in the typically uneven, frustrating, confusing, and not always successful manner, the symptoms generally become increasingly evident. Parents begin to hope that the symptoms will be short-lived and outgrown so that their child will develop normally. Unfortunately, this does not usually happen. Instead, the symptoms become more complex and intensified, while parents' energies and hopes diminish. Daily functioning, family relationships, and social interactions are all affected in various undesirable ways. Frequently parents discover that their methods for managing their child's behavior and reducing failure experiences are not effective. They soon begin to perceive the SLD child's symptoms as they would those of a chronic illness, as something unpleasant, which must be endured because it cannot be changed. The entire situation may seem impossible to change and equally impossible to cope with. Parents may respond to this apparent dilemma with feelings of frustration and anger or may develop feelings of guilt and depression as they search for explanations or imagine that they may have caused the problems.

It is possible to change the SLD child's symptoms. Sometimes the symptoms can be entirely eliminated if they are not too severe and appropriate kinds of learning experiences and support are provided. Sometimes the symptoms can only be reduced in severity or frequency, but to a level more tolerable for both the child and others. If parents, teachers, and other specialists collaborate to provide the child with a prescriptive program, they will be playing a vital role in eliminating or at least reducing the SLD child's symptoms.

Learning takes time and changes may occur slowly, depending upon the child's level of learning ability. The child may need to test the limits and merits of a behavior management system. The child may be reluctant to give up immature behavioral responses for more appropriate ones. A behavior management technique should not be abandoned if immediate progress is not evident.

Some behaviors may improve quickly in response to a well-structured environment. Remove the structure too quickly, however, and the previous behaviors will probably return. With structure, frequent repetition of the improved behaviors enables the child to learn these more desirable responses. Eventually, as these improved behaviors become more or less habitual, structure can be reduced.

Regressions may occur. When the child is under exceptional stress, fatigued, or physically ill, previous response patterns may recur. If so, don't feel as though all is lost or your efforts have been in vain. Instead, increased support, structure, and patience may be required to help the child get through the regression and return to the previously higher or better controlled level of functioning. The child might be helped to regain control more quickly if your own behavior is consistent and controlled.

At times you will make mistakes. After a problem situation is over you may realize that you should have handled it differently. These mistakes are not catastrophic. Generally the child will recognize the basic consistency and support you provide and be able to absorb the "mistakes." Openly admitting your mistakes and discussing them with the child at appropriate times communicates the message that adults are not infallible, that making mistakes does not make a person inadequate (as the child might feel about himself), and that you care enough about the child to examine and improve your responses. What an excellent role model you will be providing for the child because of your "mistakes."

Although it may be difficult, try not to take the child's behavior personally. Try to maintain some degree of objectivity. The child's behavior stems from his skill weaknesses and needs and is not always deliberately designed to torment you. This is not to imply that your own behavior or attitude should be aloof or indifferent. You need to remain a caring person, but avoid getting caught up in power struggles. Remember that a firm, calm attitude communicates more "authority" than yelling and losing control of feelings.

The SLD child can be helped to develop skills and behavior patterns that are at or near age-level expectancies by means of: (a) structure, limits, and consistency; (b) prescriptive learning experiences; (c) an accepting and supportive environment; (d) positive role models; (e) the coordinated efforts of parents and various professionals; and (f) maturation and time. As this goal is approached, daily experiences with the child will become more enjoyable. As the child's self-image improves from increasingly successful experiences, the adult's perception of the child may also improve. If all goes well, the SLD child and his behavior will gradually change from impossible to tolerable or even lovable.

To conclude, a summary list of basic recommendations is offered concerning the behavior management of SLD children:

1. Become aware of the child's strengths and weaknesses. Be sure that your expectations and the requirements of a task or situation are within the child's present range of ability.

2. Be tolerant of daily fluctuations in skill efficiency. A situation might be handled well today, but present difficulties tomorrow. We all have times when we cannot function at peak efficiency; the SLD child experiences this more often.

3. Set the stage to ensure as many successful experiences as possible through the use of structure, support, and consistency.

4. Recognize that the child's misbehaviors generally reflect skill weaknesses. Don't allow dislike for the child's behavior to be communicated as dislike for the child.

5. Be sure that the child understands what is expected. In a slow, calm, and concise manner, explain how you expect the child to perform or behave in a particular situation. Avoid vague statements such as, "I want you to be a good boy." Instead, offer specific guidelines such as, "Walk when you're in the house, don't run." Demonstrate your expectations if necessary so that the child can hear and see what is expected.

6. Offer praise and rewards for appropriate behavior and effort; do not simply rely upon discipline for inappropriate behavior. Recognition for appropriate behavior is often more effective than discipline for inappropriate behavior. The specific discipline or consequence for a particular misbehavior should be selected so that the cause-effect relationship is clear to the child.

7. Do not be surprised if the child tests the limits of a situation to see if you mean what you say. Maintain consistency in applying the consequences whenever the limits of acceptable behavior have been broken.

8. Work at developing a positive relationship with the child. The fact that you are the child's parent or teacher (or other helping person) is not enough. This does not mean to give in to the child's demands, but to communicate acceptance, respect, understanding, and a desire to help. This includes enforcing consequences to help the child learn to respect limits.

9. Try to anticipate behavior problems on the basis of your previous experiences with the child. Learn to recognize the early stages of a behavior problem and do whatever seems reasonably indicated to help the child maintain effective control. Preventing an emotional blow-up or failure is usually more therapeutic for the child (and for everyone else) than helping the child regain control after the problem behavior has occurred.

10. Stay sufficiently in tune with the child's development and progress. This will help you know when the child is ready for additional responsibilities, more stressful situations, or less structure. If a newly presented change or responsibility cannot be handled successfully, evaluate the problem. Is the change or increased responsibility too great? Is increased structure or support needed to help the child get through the new experience successfully? Must certain skills be developed or strengthened further before any changes are introduced?

11. Parents, teachers, and other specialists should collaborate in providing the child with prescriptively appropriate experiences to assist in the development of prerequisite skills for successful living.

12. Remember, you have needs and feelings, too. Arrange opportunities for personal gratification through advanced planning, schedules or routines, and back-up support from others. You must receive sufficient gratification of your needs and feelings in order to remain effective in your prolonged and arduous efforts to help the SLD child assume his or her rightful place in society.

Bibliography

BOOKS

Adamson, W. C., & K. K. Adamson (Eds.) *A Handbook for Specific Learning Disabilities.* New York: Gardner Press, 1979. This book is written for educators, clinicians, and concerned parents. It provides practical information about the assessment and remediation of specific learning disabilities and the roles of various professionals who must participate in the process.

Battin, R. *Speech and Language Delay: A Home Training Program.* Springfield, IL: Charles C Thomas, 1978. This book will help parents establish a home program for remediating delayed speech and language skills in children. There is information on speech and language development, causes for the delay, and various training techniques.

Consilia, Sr. M. *The Non-Coping Child.* Novato, CA: Academic Therapy Publications, 1978. A comprehensive description of techniques for diagnostic and prescriptive teaching. Includes explanations of the physical relationship between sensation, perception, conceptualization, and health of the learning disabled child.

Cruickshank, W. M. *Learning Disabilities in Home, School, and Community.* Syracuse: Syracuse University Press, 1977. This book gives parents and teachers an overview of the issues germane to the adjustment of their learning disabled children.

Feingold, B. F. *Why Your Child Is Hyperactive.* New York: Random House, 1975. This book is written by an allergist who describes the learning and behavioral problems caused by food additives, such as artificial colors and flavorings. A special K-P diet is suggested to help this condition.

Hammill, D. D., & N. R. Bartel. *Teaching Children with Learning and Behavior Problems.* (2nd ed.) Boston: Allyn and Bacon, 1978. Reviews roles and duties of teachers in the management of children with school-related problems, assessment techniques, instructional methods, specific materials, and resources.

Haring, N. G., & B. Bateman, *Teaching the Learning Disabled Child.* Englewood Cliffs, NJ: Prentice-Hall, 1977. A methods book which emphasizes the teaching of learning disabled children. Reviews learning theories and remediation approaches.

Johnson, S. W., & R. L. Marasky. *Learning Disabilities.* Boston: Allyn and Bacon, 1977. Provides a comprehensive review of various issues in learning disabilities, with the focus on remediation.

Lewis, R. S. *The Other Child Grows Up.* Scranton, PA: Times Book, 1977. Discusses the history, diagnosis, and causes of learning disabilities. The benefits of special education are presented.

Meade, J. G. *The Rights of Parents and the Responsibilities of Schools.* Cambridge, MA: Educators Publishing Service, 1978. Describes Public Law 94-142 and Public Law 93-112, Section 504 and lists information centers and associations that serve handicapped populations. Also includes bibliography of relevant books and directories for parents and teachers.

Osman, Betty B. *Learning Disabilities: A Family Affair.* New York: Random House, 1979. This book is designed to help parents and professionals recognize early signs and symptoms of learning disabilities. Implications for home, school, and social situations are discussed.

Rosner, J. *Helping Children Overcome Learning Difficulties: A Step-By-Step Guide for Parents and Teachers.* New York: Walker and Company, 1979. A guide for teaching learning disabled children to analyze, organize, and associate information more easily. Contains er Sargent

) Boston:

Vincent/

ivities and assignments to teach reading, math,
riting.

swers: *The Learning Disabled Child.* Rockville,
tute for Mental Health, 1978. Describes the
ions of learning disabilities. Explores the child's
d social problems, and suggestions for parents

ills *in the Classroom.* Columbus, OH: Cedars
suggestions for teaching social skills in ways
eved to learn these behaviors in their natural

ns.
al Children.

n," *Federal*

Handicapped
Disabilities,"
977.

ion *of Learning Disabilities: A Handbook of
source Programs.* Belmont, CA: Fearon-
74. Illustrates specific learning objectives
us for their accomplishment. Focus is on
motor development, sensory motor integra-
skills, language development, conceptual

e. *Communicative Disorders: A Handbook
Intervention.* St. Louis, MO: C. V. Mosby
mmunication development and disorders,
d preventing these disorders, and remedia-

Learning Dis-
42, Millburn,

nation Center
13.

1e is *a Learning Place: A Parent's Guide to*
ton: Little, Brown, 1976. The authors,
d children, give practical information on
e home and on activities in the areas of
nd academic skills.

amps that offer programs for children
well as children with other handicaps.

for the Learning Disabled. (8th ed.)
Publications, 1979–80.

The Directory for Exceptional Children. (9th ed.) Boston: Port
   Publishers, 1981–82.
The Guide to Summer Camps and Summer Schools. (21st ed.
   Porter Sargent Publishers, 1979–80.
The Vincent/Curtis Educational Register. (39th ed.) Boston
   Curtis Publishers, 1979–80.

JOURNALS AND PERIODICALS

Academic Therapy. Novato, CA: Academic Therapy Publication
Exceptional Children. Reston, VA: The Council for Exception
Journal of Learning Disabilities. Chicago: Professional Press.
Public Law 94-142: "Education of Handicapped Childre
   Register 42, no. 163, Tuesday, August 23, 1977.
Public Law 94-142: "Assistance to States for Education of
   Children: Procedures for Evaluating Specific Learning
   Federal Register 42, no. 250, Thursday, December 29, 1
The Exceptional Parent. Boston: Psy-Ed Corporation.

NEWSLETTERS

*Perceptions: The Newsletter for Parents of Children with
   abilities.* Millburn, N.J.: Perceptions, Inc., P. O. Box
   N.J. 07041.
The Closer Look Report. Washington: The National Infor
   for the Handicapped, Box 1492, Washington, D.C. 200

Glossary

Brain injury. Any structural damage to the brain, whether by surgery, accident, or disease. Sources of diagnostic data include a neurological assessment, EEG (brain wave test), or selected psychological tests.

Cause-effect relationship. A causal connection between two events or experiences; one occurs invariably with the other. The connection between a person's behavior, the reasons for the behavior, and the effects of the behavior.

Developmental aphasia. An impaired ability to understand or use language due to damage or a malfunctioning of the central nervous system. Sources of diagnostic data include selected psychological tests, various speech and language tests, and neurological assessment.

Developmental levels. Children develop physical, emotional, and cognitive skills at different rates. While the majority of children may develop a particular skill (walking, talking, reading) within a similar age range, some children develop the same skills earlier than usual and some later. If a particular skill typically develops around age three, for example, but a child does not develop that skill until age five, the child is developmentally at the three-year level for that particular skill.

Distractibility. An observable characteristic of a person whose attention is easily drawn to extraneous stimuli, making it difficult to focus attention on a task or situation.

Due process hearing. A formal hearing held before a state appointed, impartial hearing officer to resolve a disagreement between a school district and parents concerning the evaluation, identification, or educational placement of a student.

Dyslexia. Reading disability. Sources of diagnostic data include diagnostic reading tests and selected psychological tests.

Fine motor skills. Those skills which depend upon the coordination of small muscles, as in fingers, and which usually involve dexterity.

Gross motor skills. Those skills which depend upon the coordination of large muscles, as in arms and legs, and which usually involve strength and endurance.

Hearing handicap. A hearing loss from mild (hard of hearing) to severe (deaf), as determined by an audiometric evaluation (hearing test).

Hyperactivity. An observable activity level or restlessness which is greater than that normally expected at a particular age.

Individualized education program (IEP). A written plan which describes the special education program and related services to meet the individual needs of an exceptional student.

Impulsiveness. An observable characteristic of a person who reacts without thought; immediate response to an impulse.

Local educational agency (LEA). The local school district responsible for the educational program of the student.

Least restrictive environment. The educational placement which meets the student's needs and abilities, while allowing that student to be educated with non-handicapped students to the maximum extent that is appropriate.

Mental retardation. Intelligence levels which are below an IQ of 69 as measured by an individual test of intelligence, such as one of the Wechsler scales.

Minimal brain dysfunction. A malfunctioning of the central nervous system which produces learning and behavioral disabilities in spite of at least near average ability. Sources of diagnostic data include selected psychological and educational tests, and a neurological assessment.

Motor handicap. Impaired coordination of muscles. Sources of diagnostic data include selected psychological tests and a motor skills assessment by a physical therapist or an adapted physical education specialist.

Perceptual handicap. An impaired ability to perceive information accurately through one or more of the senses due to a malfunctioning of the central nervous system. Sources of diagnostic data include selected psychological, educational, and speech and language tests.

Perceptual-motor integration. The ability to translate a visual or auditory stimulus into an appropriate motor response: e.g., following a verbal command to do something; drawing a picture of an object being observed.

Perseveration. An observable characteristic of a person to repeat a thought or action without an apparent stimulus.

Public Law 94-142. The Education for All Handicapped Children Act of 1975.

Role playing. In psychotherapy, having the client act out or imitate the role of someone else in a contrived situation to reveal how the client perceives that person's role, e.g., having a child act out the role of his mother disciplining him.

Rote memory. Recall of information which was learned in a mechanical, routine manner through repetition but without understanding.

Specific learning disability (SLD). A disorder in one or more of the basic psychological processes involved in understanding or in using language, spoken or written, which may manifest itself in an imperfect ability to listen, think, speak, read, write, spell, or to do mathematical calculations. Sources of diagnostic data include selected psychological, educational, and speech and language tests.

Stimulus (pl. stimuli). Anything that arouses or incites a reaction. The reaction may involve thought, activity, or feelings.

Structure. The calibrated and consistent use of appropriate guidance and support, specific limits and consequences, predetermined schedules and procedures, and simplified experiences to provide a child with optimal success.

Therapeutic discipline. Methods of training which (1) attempt to correct, mold, or strengthen a child's behavioral responses, (2) are prescriptively selected to be relevant to the child's developmental levels, and (3) are applied in a manner which reflects empathic understanding of the child's needs.

Twenty/twenty (20/20) vision. Normal visual acuity.

Visual acuity. Ability to discriminate fine differences in visual detail.

Visual handicap. Impaired visual acuity as determined from an evaluation by a vision specialist.

Visual-motor skills. Those skills which depend upon the coordination of vision with muscular movements.

Index